S0-AZZ-756

Thomas Jefferson's

Flower Garden

at Monticello

# THOMAS JEFFERSON'S

# AT MONTICELLO

Published for the THOMAS JEFFERSON MEMORIAL FOUNDATION, In

# FLOWER GARDEN

EDWIN M. BETTS *and* HAZLEHURST BOLTON PERKINS
Revised and Enlarged by PETER J. HATCH

by the UNIVERSITY PRESS OF VIRGINIA    *Charlottesville*

Copyright © 1971, 1986 by the

Thomas Jefferson Memorial Foundation, Inc.

*First published 1941*
*Third edition 1986*
*University Press of Virginia*

Library of Congress Cataloging-in-Publication Data
Betts, Edwin Morris, 1892–1958.
  Thomas Jefferson's flower garden at Monticello.

  Bibliography: p.
    1. Jefferson, Thomas, 1743–1826—Homes and haunts—
Virginia.  2. Monticello (Va.)  3. Gardens—Virginia.
I. Perkins, Hazlehurst Bolton.  II. Hatch, Peter J.,
1949–  .  III. Thomas Jefferson Memorial Foundation,
Inc.  IV. Title.
E332.74.B48   1986     973.4'6'0924       86-5613
ISBN: 0–8139–1087–0

Printed in the United States of America

*Dedicated to the*

*members of the*

*Garden Club of Virginia*

*who made possible the restoration of*

*the flower garden at Monticello*

*the home of Thomas Jefferson*

# Preface

THE flower garden at Monticello is different from other flower gardens of Virginia. Although Jefferson was familiar with the gardens of Virginia, especially those at Williamsburg, they had little influence on him in the landscaping of his own grounds. On seeing the garden for the first time the visitor is surprised at the absence of boxwood. This shrub, which plays such an important part in restored gardens of Virginia, appears not to have been used at all by Jefferson at Monticello. No mention is made of it in his Garden Book, memoranda, or letters. On account of this, the Restoration Committees have not planted boxwood in the garden. For the same reason, other well-known flowers and shrubs, such as sweet alyssum and crape myrtle, which were grown in Virginia gardens of Jefferson's time, have not been used. But the flowers, shrubs, and trees which Jefferson did have at Monticello were numerous, and many of them were beautiful. He introduced new plants into this section of Virginia and carried on a kind of experimental garden.

Jefferson's plans, used in restoring the flower garden, date from about 1807. By this time he had decided definitely to retire at the end of his second term as president and was making many plans for his garden. It was during this period that the gravel "round-about walk" and the oval and circular flower beds around the house were laid out, the weeping willows were planted between the shrubs around the semioval in front of the house, and the first mention was made of "setting stones." Since Jefferson left several plans of his gardens and the names of plants that he grew in them, and in some instances the bed or border where they were planted, the restoration of the garden has been carried out with great accuracy.

The sketch which follows tells something of Jefferson's interest in gardens and plants, the laying out and building of his garden at Monticello, and what the Garden Club of Virginia, through its committees, has accomplished in restoring this garden.

Two committees cooperated in the restoration of the garden, one from the Garden Club of Virginia, and the other, the Restoration Committee, from the Thomas Jefferson Memorial Foundation:

The Committee from the Garden Club of Virginia:

Mrs. William Allan Perkins, Albemarle Garden Club, *Chairman*
Mrs. Delos Kidder, Rivanna Garden Club
Mrs. William R. Massie, Albemarle Garden Club
Mrs. Fairfax Harrison, General Chairman of Restoration Committee of the Garden Club of Virginia

The Committee from the Thomas Jefferson Memorial Foundation:

Fiske Kimball, *Chairman*
Milton Grigg
Edwin M. Betts

We are especially grateful to Mr. Thomas L. Rhodes, manager of Monticello, for his interest and cooperation in the restoration work; to Mr. Garland A. Wood, landscape gardener, of Richmond, Virginia, for scale drawings of beds, borders, and walks, and for assisting in the arrangement of plants; to the Massachusetts Historical Society for permission to reproduce three of Jefferson's original plans; to the Historical Society of Pennsylvania for permission to use Jefferson's plan of his flower garden of 1807; to the Alderman Library, University of Virginia, for many courtesies; and to Dr. Fiske Kimball for permission to use material from his publications.

E. M. B.

H. B. P.

# Note to the Third Edition

The restoration of the gardens and grounds at Monticello exactly as Jefferson planned and laid them out has been reflected on the pages of this important handbook, *Thomas Jefferson's Flower Garden at Monticello*. The first edition (1941) and second edition (1971) were compiled by the late Jefferson scholar Professor Edwin Morris Betts and the eminent and lovable gardener Hazelhurst Bolton Perkins. It was Professor Betts and Mrs. Perkins who contributed so mightily to the restoration of the grounds and gardens under the generous hand of the ladies of the Garden Club of Virginia. It is highly fitting that a young scholar, Peter Hatch, Superintendent of Grounds at Monticello, has joined hands with his predecessors by revising this valuable record of Monticello's gardens. Monticello has been fortunate in having its research and restoration so ably executed and reported. One sincerely believes that Mr. Jefferson would enjoy his gardens and grounds in the 1980s just as he did during his lifetime. He would find little changed.

JAMES A. BEAR, JR.

# Acknowledgments

I would like to thank three people for making special contributions to the third edition. Cinder Stanton, Research Associate at Monticello, reviewed the original Jefferson material to make more accurate transcriptions. Peggy Newcomb, Assistant Gardens and Grounds Superintendent, helped compile the information for the flower annotation, and John C. MacGregor IV of Pasadena, California, assisted in the identification of Jefferson's roses.

PETER HATCH

# Contents

Thomas Jefferson's

Flower Garden

at Monticello

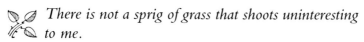 *There is not a sprig of grass that shoots uninteresting to me.*

JEFFERSON TO MARTHA JEFFERSON RANDOLPH (1790)

# Early Planning and Planting

*Of prospect I have a rich profusion and offering itself at
every point of the compas. Mountains distant & near,
smooth & shaggy, single & in ridges, a little river hiding
itself among the hills so as to shew in lagoons only, cultivated grounds under the eye and two small villages. To
prevent a satiety of this is the principal difficulty. It may be
successively offered, & in different portions through vistas,
or which will be better, between thickets so disposed as to
serve for vistas, with the advantage of shifting the scene as
you advance on your way.*

JEFFERSON TO WILLIAM HAMILTON (1806)

JEFFERSON'S interest in flowers and gardening began
early in his life. While still living at Shadwell, his boyhood
home, he kept a record of the planting, blooming, and dis-
appearance of flowers in the family garden and in the woods
and fields. That he took an active part in gardening is shown
by the many entries about plants in his Garden Book.

The first page from his Garden Book, in which he jotted
down garden notes from 1766 to 1824, shows this early interest:

Shadwell

1766

Mar. 30. Purple hyacinth begins to bloom.
Apr. 6. Narcissus and Puckoon open.
   13. Puckoon flowers fallen.
   16. A bluish colored, funnel-formed flower in lowgrounds in bloom.
   30. Purple flag blooms. Hyacinth & Narcissus gone.
May 4. Wild honeysuckle in our woods open.—also the Dwarf flag & Violet.
   7. Blue flower in lowgrounds vanished.
   11. The purple flag, Dwarf flag, Violet & wild Honeysuckle still in bloom.

When Jefferson moved to Monticello in November 1770, he was not only an experienced gardener but one who had observed gardens and gardening in many places. He knew well the plans and plants of the gardens at Williamsburg, where he had spent most of the time between 1759 and 1770, first as a student at the College of William and Mary and then studying law and practicing in the General Court. He had visited the gardens at Tuckahoe, Rosewell, Ampthill, Eppington, and The Forest and also gardens at Fredericksburg, Annapolis, Philadelphia, and New York.

While on a visit to Annapolis in the spring of 1766, he wrote to his friend John Page, "The situation of this place is extremely beautiful. . . . The houses are in general better than those in Williamsburgh, but the gardens more indifferent." Here is a young man, at the age of twenty-three, observing gardens, not as an amateur, but as a connoisseur.

Jefferson's library contained many books on gardening, botany, and agriculture. Of the books on gardening, *Observations on Modern Gardening* by Thomas Whately, Philip Miller's *The Gardener's Dictionary,* and *The American Gardener's Calendar* by Bernard McMahon apparently influenced him most in planning and laying out his garden at Monticello. He probably owned a copy of Whately's book before he went to Paris in 1784. If not, he bought it soon afterwards, for in 1786 when he made a tour of some English gardens, he carried Whately's book with him, observing most of the gardens described in it. Whately's ideas of naturalistic gardening fascinated Jefferson, and he incorporated many of them in his garden at Monticello. Such features as "gravelled walks" and "oval raised beds, cultivated, and flowers among the shrubs," all became parts of his garden.

But Jefferson had ideas of his own. Monticello was situated on a mountaintop, a location where no pioneer in young America had hitherto ventured to build his house. There were new problems to solve, problems that neither Whately in England nor anyone in this country had encountered. That Jefferson solved them with satisfaction and great interest shows again his versatility.

In his Pocket Account Book for 1771, Jefferson put down interesting tentative plans for landscaping and beautifying the grounds of Monticello. Although some of these landscaping schemes were fanciful, and probably never implemented, many of them were carried out. The marquis de Chastellux, who visited Jefferson in the spring of 1782, found a score of deer in his park. He wrote of them, "They soon become very tame. . . . He enjoys feeding them with Indian corn, of which they are very fond, and which they eat out of his hand." The "benches or seats of rock or turf," mentioned in his plans, he later called "setting stones" and placed about the grounds. Here are some of his plans:

At the spring on the North side of the park.

A few feet below the spring level the ground 40, or 50 f. sq. Let the water fall from the spring in the upper level over a terrace in the form of a cascade. Then conduct it along the foot of the terrace to the Western side of the level, where it may fall into a cistern under a temple, from which it may go off by the western border till it falls over another terrace at the Northern or lower side. . . .

. . . Plant trees of Beech and Aspen about it. Open a vista to the millpond, the river, road, &c. Qu. if a view of the neighboring town would have a good effect? Intersperse in this and every other part of the ground (except the environs of the Burying ground) abundance of Jessamine, Honeysuckle, sweet briar &c. Under the temple an Aeolian harp where it may be concealed as well as covered from the weather.

.    .    .    .    .

### The Ground in General.

Thin the trees. Cut out stumps and undergrowth. Remove old trees and other rubbish except where they may look well. Cover the whole with grass. Intersperse Jesamine, honeysuckle, sweetbriar, and even hardy flowers which may not require attention. Keep in it deer, rabbits, Peacocks, Guinea poultry, pidgeons &c. Let it be an asylum for hares, squirrels, pheasants, partridges and every other wild animal (except those of prey.) Court them to it by laying food for them in proper places. Procure a buck elk, to be as it were Monarch of the wood; but keep him shy, that his appearance may not lose it's effect by too much familiarity. A buffalo might perhaps be confined also. Inscriptions in various places on the bark of trees or metal plates, suited to the character or expression of the particular spot. Benches or seats of rock or turf passim.

### The Open Ground on the West. A shrubbery.

Shrubs. (not exceeding a growth of 10. f.) Alder. — Bastard indigo. flowering. Amorpha. — Barberry — Cassioberry. Cassine. — Chinquapin — Jersey-Tea. F. Ceanothus. —

Dwarf cherry. F. Cerasus. 5. — Clethra — Cockspur haw-thorn, or haw. Crataegus. 4. — Laurel. — Scorpion Sena. Emerus. — Hazel. — Althea F. — Callicarpa. — Rose — Wild Honeysuckle — Sweet briar — Ivy.

Trees. Lilac. — wild cherry — Dogwood — Redbud — Horse chesnut — Catalpa — Magnolia — Mulberry — Lo-cust — Honeysuckle — Jessamine. — Elder. — Poison oak — Haw.

Climbing shrubby plants. Trumpet flower — Jasmine — Honeysuckle

Evergreens. Holly — Juniper — Laurel — Magnolia — Yew.

Hardy perennial flowers. Snapdragon — Daisy — Lark-spur — Gilliflower — Sunflower. — Lilly — Mallow — Flower de luce — Everlasting pea — Piony — Poppy — Pas-que flower — Goldy-lock. Trollius. — Anemone — Lilly of the valley — Primrose — Periwincle — Violet. — Flag

Although Jefferson began leveling the top of Monticello mountain in 1768 and moved there in 1770, little was done in laying out a definitely planned flower garden until 1807. He was away from Monticello for a considerable part of the time, except for short visits, from his departure to France in 1784 until he retired in 1809. Most of the landscaping before 1807 consisted of building roads, clearing land, and planting new shrubs and trees. These plants came from nurseries, from various parts of the country, and from abroad. For many years his friend André Thouin, superintendent of the Jardin des Plantes, at Paris, sent him seeds and exotic plants from Europe. Of these he planted some at Monticello and sent some to botanical gardens and private gardens throughout the country.

While he was in Washington, Jefferson's favorite trips were to nurseries and to those people who were interested in growing plants. Mrs. Margaret Bayard Smith, of Washington, a friend of Jefferson's, wrote an interesting account of these trips:

> There were two nursery-gardens he took peculiar delight in, partly on account of their romantic and picturesque location and the beautiful rides that led to them, but chiefly because he discovered in their proprietors, an uncommon degree of scientific information, united with an enthusiastic love of their occupation. Mr. Mayne [Main], a shrewd, intelligent, warm hearted Scotchman, rough as he was in his manners and appearance, could not be known, without being person- ally liked. It was he who introduced into this section of our country, the use of the American Thorn for hedges. This was the favorite, though not exclusive object of his zealous industry. Rare fruits and flowers were his pride and delight: this similarity of tastes made Mr. Jefferson find peculiar plea- sure, in furnishing him with foreign plants and seeds, and in visiting his plantations on the high banks of the Potomac.

It was from Thomas Main that Jefferson bought the thorn plants that enclosed his two orchards and the vegetable gar- den. He also furnished Jefferson with a large variety of shrubs and trees which were planted at Monticello.

A portion of a letter written by Jefferson from Philadel- phia, March 22, 1798, to his son-in-law Thomas Mann Ran- dolph gives an insight into the kinds of plants he ordered from nurseries and his knowledge of their scientific names. It also shows with what care his plants were sent to Monti- cello and the detailed instructions for planting them. The Mr. Jefferson mentioned in this letter was Thomas Jefferson's agent in Richmond, Virginia. The plants were sent by boat up the James and Rivanna rivers to Milton, a small but then thriving town on the Rivanna River near Monticello.

I have just had put on board the sloop Sally, Capt. Potter for Richmond, a harpsichord for Maria, and a box of plants, which I shall desire Mr. Jefferson to forward up the river without delay. The plants are distinguished by numbers as follow.

No. 1. Rhododendron maximum 3. plants. To be planted in the Nursery.

2. Scotch pines. 3. plants ⎫ to be planted among the
3. Norway firs. 2. do. ⎪ Kentuckey Coffee trees in
4. Balm of Gilead. 2. do. ⎬ an open space between the
6. Dwarf Ewe 3. do. ⎭ Pride of China trees & the
Grove, about S. W. & by W. from the house. They may be planted within 20. feet of one another; therefore I suppose there will be space enough in the place I describe to receive them all, without disturbing the Coffee trees.

5. Juniper. 3. plants. To be planted on the upper Roundabout between or in continuation of the Arborvitaes & Cedars.

7. Aesculus Virginica. yellow Horse ⎫ on the
                chestnut  1. plant ⎪ Slope
8.        hybrida    variegated  1. do. ⎪ leading
9.        Pavia      Scarlet     1. do. ⎬ from the
10.       Alba       white       1. do. ⎪ Pride of
11. Sugar maple   2. plants ⎪ China
12. Balsam poplars. 3. do. ⎭ trees
down to the shops, among the Catalpas, Crabapple trees &c. wherever there are vacant spaces.

13. Viburnum opulifolium. bush cranberry. 3. plants. in the curran or gooseberry squares.

14. Alpine strawberries ⎫ in new & separate beds in the
15. Chili strawberries  ⎭ garden. Both of these kinds are immensely valuable.

16. Antwerp raspberry. Twenty odd plants I expect. In some new row by themselves. It has the reputation

of being among the finest fruits in the world.
Peruvian winter grass. Many roots of this are
packed in among the plants. It is a most valuable
grass for winter grazing. John had better take some
favorable place under trees to set it out. The cherry
trees in the garden would be good places, if there is
not danger of too much trampling.
Many nuts of the yellow & scarlet Horse chesnut are
stuck in among the moss. John must set them out in
the nursery instantly, & before they dry.

I must ask the favor of you, the moment these things arrive
at Milton, to send to James to go for them with his waggon,
& to take a ride to Monticello, as soon as they get there, &
direct John where to plant them. He would do well perhaps
to dig his holes before hand, to mellow the earth. All the
trees to be well staked, & the numbers preserved.

The Garden Book and memoranda recorded the planting
of numerous seeds and flowers, but if they were planted in
any planned flower garden before 1807, there is no available
record of it. Even the vegetable garden, on the top south side
of the mountain, was not completed until after 1809.

Plans for the house drawn by Jefferson before he went to
Paris show places for trees paralleling the terraces of the
house, but there is no record showing what trees were
planted. The earliest known plan for the house and grounds,
begun about 1772 and probably finished by additions to it
around 1808 or 1809, however, does indicate the location and
the names of certain shrubs to be planted around the semioval
in front of the house. Shrubs were to alternate with trees in
an unusual design. The shrubs were planted some time before
the trees, as is shown by a memorandum left for Edmund
Bacon, his overseer, around 1808, or 1809, "Plant weeping
willows in the semi-circle in N.E. front one half way between

each two shrubs." The plan also shows that in May 1783, European ("Italian") larch, Chinese arborvitae, *Thuja occidentalis,* "Newfoundland spruce" *(Picea mariana),* and balsam ("balm of Gilead') fir were planted on the first roundabout near the North Pavilion.

People who came to Monticello to visit Jefferson, and those who have come since his death, were enraptured by the vistas unfolding in all directions. Many of them have left illuminating descriptions of their impressions. In June 1796, at the time Jefferson was remodeling his house, the duc de La Rochefoucauld-Liancourt, the patriotic French nobleman, came to visit him. He wrote of the prospect:

> Mr. Jefferson's house commands one of the most extensive prospects you can meet with. On the east side, the front of the building, the eye is not checked by any object, since the mountain on which the house is seated commands all the neighboring heights as far as the Chesapeake. The Atlantic might be seen, were it not for the greatness of the distance, which renders the prospect impossible. On the right and left the eye commands the extensive valley that separates the Green, South, and West Mountains from the Blue-Ridge, and has no other bounds but these high mountains, of which, on a clear day, you discern the chain on the right upwards of a hundred miles, far beyond the James River; and on the left as far as Maryland, on the other side of the Potomac. Through some intervals, formed by the irregular summits of the Blue Mountains, you discover the Peaked Ridge, a chain of mountains placed between the Blue and North Mountains, another more distant ridge. But in the back part the prospect is soon interrupted by a mountain more elevated than that on which the house is seated. The bounds of the view on this point, at so small a distance, form a pleasant resting-place, as the immensity of prospect it enjoys is,

Observations from a spur of the mountain back of Monticello. Aug. 4. 1772.

Willis's mountain bore S. 2° E.

Slate river mountains, highest point S. 29° W.
 their Eastern end, running low, bore S. 21. W.

Monticello, then bore N. 18° E.

Observed from Monticello. same day.

Willis's mountain S. 1° E

Intersection of the back mountain with horizon S. 12° W.

Dwelling house fronts S. 65° W & N. 65° E.

Little Piney mountain bears from N.W. corner of Kitchen S. 33° 45' E. 349 yards

The Slate quarry bears from Monticello S. 32. E.

the mountains seen from Elkhill are from N. 77. W. to N. 28. W.

Elk-hill bears from Monticello S. 18 E.

Plan of house and gardens drawn by Jefferson about 1772 with additions made about 1808 or 1809 (*Courtesy of the Massachusetts Historical Society*)

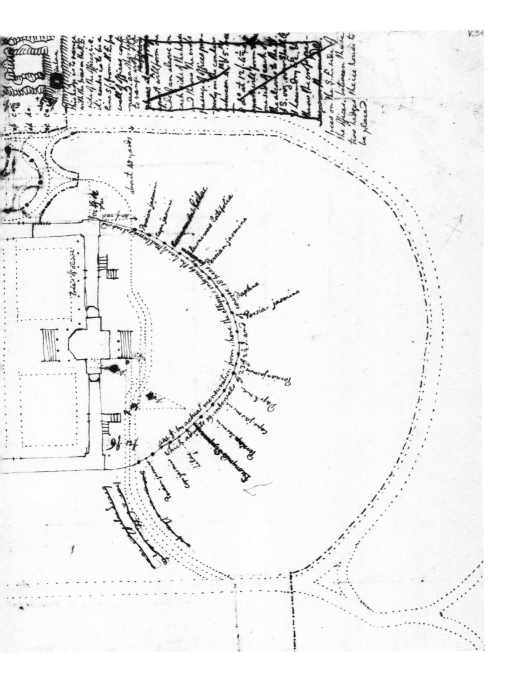

perhaps, already too vast. A considerable number of cultivated fields, houses, and barns, enliven and variegate the extensive landscape, still more embellished by the beautiful
and diversified forms of mountains, in the whole chain of
which not one resembles another. The aid of fancy is, however, required to complete the enjoyment of this magnificent
view; and she must picture to us those plains and mountains
such as population and culture will render them in a greater
or smaller number of years. The disproportion existing between the cultivated lands and those which are still covered
with forests as ancient as the globe, is at present much too
great; and even when that shall have been done away, the eye
may perhaps further wish to discover a broad river, a great
mass of water—destitute of which, the grandest and most
extensive prospect is ever destitute of an embellishment req-
uisite to render it completely beautiful.

 *I never before knew the full value of trees. My house is
entirely embosomed in high plane trees, with good grass
below, and under them I breakfast, dine, write, read and
receive my company. What would I not give that the trees
planted nearest round the house at Monticello were full
grown.*

JEFFERSON TO MARTHA JEFFERSON RANDOLPH (1793)

# The Climate of Monticello

*I find nothing any where else in point of climate which Virginia need envy to any part of the world. Here [northern New York] they are locked up in ice and snow for 6. months. Spring and autumn, which make a paradise of our country, are rigorous winter with them, and a Tropical summer breaks on them all at once. When we consider how much climate contributes to the happiness of our condn., by the fine sensations it excites, and the productions it is the parent of, we have reason to value highly the accident of birth in such an one as that of Virginia.*

JEFFERSON TO MARTHA JEFFERSON RANDOLPH (1791)

T O JEFFERSON, tending a garden on a mountaintop, the weather was of the first importance. The amount of rainfall, the severity of the winds, the dates of first and last killing frosts, and the range in temperature occupied his attention for many years.

He began his systematic record of the weather in the year 1776 while at Philadelphia, where he had gone to attend a session of the Continental Congress, at which time he wrote the Declaration of Independence. From this date until his death he kept an almost continuous record of the weather. This record was tabulated not only at Monticello but wherever he was living.

During his frequent absences from Monticello, he was constantly writing to his daughters Martha and Maria, his son-in-law Thomas Mann Randolph, and his grandson Thomas Jefferson Randolph for information about the weather on his "little mountain." A comparative estimate of the weather at Monticello and where he was then living fascinated him. Their lack of enthusiasm often irritated him and a tactful scolding followed in his letters to them. These scoldings would arouse their interest for a short time only.

Writing from Philadelphia, March 9, 1791, he longs for some word as to the approach of spring at Monticello in order to compare it with spring there:

My dear Maria
    I am happy to have at length a letter of yours to answer, for that which you wrote to me Feb. 13. came to hand Feb. 28. I hope our correspondence will now be more regular, that you will be no more lazy, and I no more in the growls on that account. On the 27th. of February I saw blackbirds and Robinredbreasts, and on the 7th. of this month I heard frogs for the first time this year. Have you noted the first appearance of these things at Monticello? I hope you have, and will continue to note every appearance animal and vegetable which indicates the approach of Spring, and will communicate them to me. By these means we shall be able to compare the climates of Philadelphia and Monticello. Tell me when you shall have peas &c. up, when every thing comes to table, when you shall have the first chickens hatched, when every kind of tree blossoms, or puts forth leaves, when each kind of flower blooms.


Weather reports continued to pass between Jefferson and the household at Monticello

From Philadelphia, March 31, 1791: "The blue birds saluted us on the 17th. The weeping-willow began to leaf on the 18th. The lilac and gooseberry on the 25th. And the golden willow on the 26th."

From Monticello, May 1, 1791: "The peaches cherrys and strawberries are very big allready and there are a great number."

From Philadelphia, May 8, 1791: "April 30. the lilac blossomed. May 4. the gelderrose, Dogwood, Red bud, and Azalea were in blossom. We have still pretty constant fires here."

From Monticello, May 23, 1791: "We had strawberries here the 2d of this month and cherries I think the 9th tho they had had both some time before that at Richmond."

From Lake Champlain, New York, May 31, 1791: "Strawberries here are in the blossom, or just formed. With you I suppose the season is over. On the whole I find nothing any where else in point of climate which Virginia need envy to any part of the world."

And so the weather gossip went on, when asparagus came to the table, when magnolias bloomed, and when the first tuberoses appeared.

The weather record kept by Jefferson at Monticello was necessarily sketchy and incomplete until after his retirement in 1809 from the presidency. This mainly was owing to his long absences from the mountain. In 1810, the year following his retirement, he began a continuous weather record at Monticello, in which he noted the temperature, the direction of the winds, the date of the first and last white frost and ice, the amount of rainfall, the depth of snows, the length of time they remained on the ground, and the first arrival of many animals and plants.

At the end of seven years he made a summary of the weather recorded for the period and often referred to it in his gardening and farming operations. Some of the figures calculated in the summary are:

Minimum and maximum temperature of the whole term: 5½° and 94½°.
Average number of freezing nights and days in a winter: 50 and 10.
Fires necessary in apartments: 4 months constant, and on evening and morning of month before and after that time.
Earliest and latest frosts: October 7–26 and March 19–May 15.
Earliest and latest ice: October 24–November 15 and March 8–April 12.
Average quantity of water falling in a year: 47.218 inches.
Average number of rains in the year: 89.
Average number of fair days: 5 to the week.
Average quantity of snow: 22½ inches, covering the ground 22 days.
Average number of days each wind prevailed through the year: N. 61, N.E. 29, E. 15, S.E. 16, S. 60, S.W. 66, W. 47, N.W. 71.

The summary also gave the first appearance of many plants and animals, some of which are listed here:

| | | | | |
|---|---|---|---|---|
| The Red Maple comes into blossom from | Feb. | 18 to | March | 27 |
| The Almond | " | Mar. | 6 to Apr. | 5 |
| The Peach | " | Mar. | 9 to " | 4 |
| The Shad arrives | " | Mar. | 28 to " | 18 |
| The Lilac blossoms | " | Apr. | 1 " | 28 |
| The Dogwood blossoms | " | Apr. | 3 " | 22 |
| The Fringe tree blooms | " | Apr. | 27 May | 5 |
| Fire flies appear | " | May | 8 to | |

# Water for a Mountaintop

*Nymph of the grot, these sacred springs I keep.*
*And to the murmur of these waters sleep:*
*Ah! spare my slumbers! gently tread the cave!*
*And drink in silence, or in silence lave!*

ALEXANDER POPE, QUOTED IN
THE POCKET ACCOUNT BOOK (1771)

NO PHYSICAL problem at Monticello was more difficult of solution than that of a sufficient water supply for the house, the lawns, and the gardens on top of the mountain. The problem grew with the expansion of Monticello. Jefferson had many schemes for solving it, but none worked with entire satisfaction during his life. His weather records show that the annual rainfall was not sufficient to take care of all the needs. The sources of water supply were the natural springs on the sides of the mountain, the well, the cisterns, and probably the fishpond near the South Pavilion.

The springs were the first source of water and were, no doubt, used more or less continuously after the well and the cisterns were in use. They certainly furnished the only water supply for the overseer's house and the other houses scattered over the sides of the mountain. The slaves, as was the custom, carried the water from the springs to the main house.

There were at least fifteen springs, ten on the south side and five on the north side of the mountain. The springs on the south side were named Bailey's, Southstone, Ned's,

Abram's, Lewis's, Nailery, Overseer's, Ragged Branch, Goodman's, and Mouth of Meadow Branch; while those on the north side were Rock, North Road Left, North Road Right Hand, Falling, and North Stone. The springs named after persons were close to the houses where these persons lived; the Overseer's Spring was close to the overseer's house. The Nailery Spring furnished water for the nail factory.

The well, 65 feet deep and located a little southeast of the rear of the South Pavilion, was dug in 1769. As a source of water supply it was rarely dependable. One year it was filled with water and "very fine," the next it was dry for months. During the dry periods the springs furnished the water.

Jefferson's record of the failure and the abundance of water in the well shows the acuteness of the problem of water supply. The record is put down with the same calm interest as his other memoranda, without any apparent anxiety over it.

> 1778. Feb. 23. The water is returned into the well at Monticello, having been now dry for 13 months. It was dug in 1769. It failed once before, to wit, in the fall of 1773, but came to the spring following. When it failed the second time as mentioned above, to wit January 1777, the succeeding spring happened to be remarkeably dry, insomuch that the rivers did not afford water to carry down tobacco &c. so that the well not being replenished in the spring, had no water all the summer of 1777.   —1789. It failed again from beginng. Oct. to beginng. Dec.   1796. Again in the fall & winter till Feb.

> dug in  1769
> failed    1773
>             1777
>             1789
>             1791
>             1796
>             1797

As late as May 1818 the well was still a problem. He wrote, "The well is found to have in it a plenty of water, and very fine. It had been several years out of use."

It was not until toward the end of his second term as president that Jefferson began plans for cisterns at Monticello. Expecting to retire to his home at the end of his second term to continue on a much larger scale his flower and vegetable gardens, he realized the need for a larger supply of water than he then commanded.

In 1808, while at home on his usual summer visit, he worked out, in his most careful manner, the roof area of the house and allotted certain gutters to carry water to each of the proposed cisterns. Four cisterns were to be built, one on each side of each covered way, near the angle with the offices.

The cisterns were built between August 1808 and April 1810. In a letter to John Adlum, written April 20, 1810, after expressing the hope that the cuttings of grapevines he had sent would live, Jefferson wrote, "their chance will be lessened because living on the top of a mountain I have not yet the command of water, which I hope to obtain this year by cisterns already prepared for saving the rain water."

In 1816 he wrote to J. F. Correa de Serra for information as to whether his observations of cisterns at Charleston could help him in the perfecting of the cisterns at Monticello. Three years later, May 15, 1819, he put down in his Account Book, "inclosed to W. J. Coffee N. York 40. D. to procure Roman cement for my cisterns." We are not told whether the Roman cement perfected his cisterns, but we may be sure that getting a sufficient water supply continued to be a major problem at Monticello.

While building cisterns, Jefferson made elaborate plans for building ponds in various places near the house for the conservation of rain water. He soon saw the impracticability of large ponds and turned his attention to smaller ones. He planned two small ponds, one near the South Pavilion and one near the North Pavilion. The records indicate that he built only one of these, the one near the South Pavilion. In his Weather Memorandum Book he wrote, "The fish pond near the S. pavilion is an Ellipsis 5. yds. wide, 10. yds. long = 40. sq. yds., very nearly. 1. yard deep = 40. cub. yds. contents." This pond, no doubt, was also used for fish and as a decorative part of the flower garden. In excavating for the pond the bricks of the bottom and parts of the sides were found, so that it was possible to restore it in its exact dimensions.

*I have often thought that if heaven had given me choice of my position and calling, it should have been on a rich spot of earth, well watered, and near a good market for the productions of the garden. No occupation is so delightful to me as the culture of the earth, and no culture comparable to that of the garden . . . I am still devoted to the garden. But though an old man, I am but a young gardener.*
JEFFERSON TO CHARLES W. PEALE (1811)

# The Greenhouse

*It [ Jefferson's suite at Monticello] consists of 3 rooms for
the library, one for his cabinet, one for his chamber, and a
green house divided from the other by glass compartments
and doors; so that the view of the plants it contains, is
unobstructed. He has not yet made his collection, having
but just finished the room, which opens on one of the terraces.*

MRS. MARGARET BAYARD SMITH (1809)

ALTHOUGH Jefferson had two nurseries for growing
his young plants and seeds, his greenhouse was only a
glassed-in piazza on the southeastern end of his house. He
made several computations for building a greenhouse on
Mulberry Row but never carried them to completion. In a
letter to William Hamilton, of Woodlands, Philadelphia,
written March 1, 1808, Jefferson explains the purposes of his
greenhouse:

> I am very thankful to you for thinking of me in the destina-
> tion of some of your fine collection. Within one year from
> this time I shall be retired to occupations of my own choice,
> among which the farm & garden will be conspicuous parts.
> My green house is only a piazza adjoining my study, because
> I mean it for nothing more than some oranges, Mimosa Far-
> nesiana & a very few things of that kind. I remember to have
> been much taken with a plant in your green house, ex-
> tremely odoriferous, and not large, perhaps 12. to 15. I.

high if I recollect rightly. You said you would furnish me a plant or two of it when I should signify that I was ready for them. Perhaps you may remember it from this circumstance, tho' I have forgot the name. This I would ask for the next spring if we can find out what it was, and some seeds of the Mimosa Farnesiana or Nilotica. The Mimosa Julibrisin or silk tree you were so kind as to send me is now safe here, about 15. I. high. I shall carry it carefully to Monticello.

By November 6, 1809, Jefferson had two *Acacia farnesiana,* one orange, and one lime in boxes in his greenhouse. But the winter temperatures proved too severe. On January 21, 1810, he recorded that the temperature in his bedroom was 37°; in the greenhouse, 21°; and outside 9¾°. Two days later the temperatures were: bedroom, 32½°; greenhouse, 20¾°; and outside, 11°. The plants in the greenhouse could not survive. By April 8, 1811, Jefferson wrote to Bernard McMahon, a Philadelphia seedsman:

> You enquire whether I have a hot house, greenhouse, or to what extent I pay attention to these things. I have only a green house, and have used that only for a very few articles. My frequent & long absences at a distant possession render my efforts even for the few greenhouse plants I aim at, abortive. During my last absence in the winter, every plant I had in it perished.

It is doubtful whether Jefferson ever grew many plants in his greenhouse. It is rarely mentioned after 1811.

The species form of French marigold (*Tagetes patula*), larkspur (*Consolida orientalis*), opium poppy (*Papaver somniferum*), and yellow snapdragon (*Antirrhinum majus*) bloom along the roundabout flower border on the west lawn.

White tulips (*Tulipa* sp.) bloom in an oval bed on the east front with the native red columbine (*Aquilegia canadensis*), Virginia bluebells (*Mertensia virginica*), and wood hyacinths (*Endymion hispanicus*).

The Florentine tulip (*Tulipa sylvestris*) is now naturalized in flower beds and on the west lawn at Monticello.

The crown imperial lily (*Fritillaria imperialis*) was ordered numerous times from Bernard McMahon, the Philadelphia nurseryman. Brown's Mountain, which Jefferson referred to as "Montalto," is in the distance.

Snapdragons (*Antirrhinum majus*) bloom in an oval bed on the east front. The Blue Ridge Mountains are in the distance.

# The Flower Beds and Borders

*May. June. July. Take up flower bulbs. Separate offsets.*
*Replant lillies. . . .*
*October. Dress flower borders & set out bulbs.*
*Oct.* ⎫ *Cover figs and tender plants. Litter Asparagus*
      ⎪ *beds.*
*Nov.* ⎬ *Plant trees, privet, thorn.*
*Dec.* ⎪ *Trim trees, vines, rasp. gooseb. currants.*
*Jan.* ⎭ *Turf. Bring in manure and trench it into hills.*

GARDEN NOTES, 1812–1813

IN THE early part of 1806, Bernard McMahon published his book, *The American Gardener's Calendar.* Soon after its publication, McMahon sent a copy of it to Jefferson. In his letter of thanks, Jefferson wrote, "From the rapid view he has taken of it & the original matter it appears to contain he has no doubt it will be found an useful aid to the friends of an art, too important to health & comfort & yet too much neglected in this country." This *Calendar* made an especial appeal to Jefferson, for it treated of American conditions of gardening. He had a number of books in his library by European authors who knew nothing about gardening conditions in America.

Jefferson and McMahon had carried on a correspondence with each other for several years before the publication of McMahon's book. Its publication started more frequent letters and the exchange and ordering of plants. In July of the same year McMahon wrote to Jefferson:

> I take the liberty of requesting your acceptance of a few Tulip roots, the bloom of which I hope will give you satisfaction: they may remain in the state I send them till October, and be then planted as directed in page 528 of my book. . . .
>
> Prefixed to the names of the Tulips you will find the following marks, significant of the Florist's divisions of the family; Bz signifies the flowers to belong to the Bizards, B. to the Bybloemens, I. to the Incomparable Verports, R. to Baguet Rigauts, r. to the Rose coloured or Cherry, & P. to the Primo Baguets.

Jefferson received the tulips on July 14. The next day he wrote McMahon:

> I recieved last night the tulip roots you were so kind as to send me, for which I return you my thanks. I shall go in a week to Monticello, whither I shall [take] them & have them planted in proper season. . . . About this time two years I shall begin to collect [plants] for that place, because I shall be able to have them attended to. At that time I shall avail myself with pleasure of your obliging offer. But my situation there & taste, will lead me to ask for curious & hardy trees, [rather] than flowers. Of the latter a few of those remarkeable either for beauty or fragrance will be the limits of my wishes.

Jefferson did not wait two years to begin collecting plants for Monticello. On January 6, 1807, he wrote to McMahon, from Washington:

> The tulip roots you were so kind as to send me, I planted at Monticello last autumn. I intend to go there the first week in March in order to commence planting out some things to be

in readiness for my kitchen & flower gardens two years
hence. A small cart will come here for such articles as I collect here, chiefly trees. But there are several articles for the
selection of which I would rather ask the assistance of your
judgment than that of any other. I note them at the foot of
my letter. If you could be so good as to furnish me with
them you would greatly oblige me. Seeds & bulbs can be so
packed as to come with perfect safety by the stage, the best
conveyance to this place because we can command it at all
times. Whether tuberous and fibrous roots can come suc-
cessfully in moss or anything else not too bulky, you are the
best judge. To give them the better chance they will be safest
with you till about the 25th. of February. Your bill for their
amount shall be immediately provided for by remit-
tance. . . .

| | |
|---|---|
| best Globe artichoke. | Auricula. |
| Antwerp raspberry | Ranunculus. |
| Alpine strawberry. | Hyacinths. |
| Lillies of a few of the best kinds. | Sweet William (Dianthus) |
| Tuberose | Wall flower |
| Crown Imperials | Marigold |
| Anemone | Saffron. |

Promptly on February 25, as Jefferson suggested, Mc-
Mahon sent the plants:

By this day's mail, I do myself the pleasure of sending you as
many of the flower-roots you were pleased to write for, as I
had at the time your kind letter came to hand; also some red
and white Globe Artichoke, Early Cabbage and a small variety of Flower-Seeds &c. which, I solicit the favour of your
accepting as a token of my best wishes.

McMahon was unable to complete Jefferson's order on February 25, so on April 2 he sent him 24 roots of double tube-

roses, 6 roots of *Sprekelia formosissima,* 90 plants of Antwerp raspberry, and 8 of alpine strawberry.

Jefferson arrived at Monticello from Washington for his usual spring visit on April 11, 1807, instead of the first week of March, as he had written to McMahon. He returned to Washington on May 13. From the eleventh to the fifteenth of April, he laid out the circular and oval flower beds near the house on the west and east lawns, and by the thirtieth they had been planted with shrubs, trees, and flowers. In the circular beds at the four corners of the house he planted 13 paper mulberries, 6 horse chestnuts, 2 tacamahac poplars, 4 purple beeches, 2 robinias, 2 chokecherries, 3 mountain ashes, 2 zanthoxylums, 1 redbud, 1 fraxinella, and 2 guelder roses. During the same interval he planted "10. willow oaks in N.W. brow of the slope, to wit from the N. Pavilion round to near the setting stones at S.W. end of level, and 12. Wild crabs from the S. to the N. pavilion near the brow of the slope."

On April 18, he planted in the oval beds around the house the following flowers, most of which had come from McMahon:

| | | |
|---|---|---|
| Dianthus | Chinensis | China pink |
| | Caryophyllus | Sweet William |
| | barbatus | Single Carnation |
| Glaucium | yellow horned poppy | |
| Ixia Chinensis | | |
| Jeffersonia binata. | | |
| Lathyrus latifolius. | Everlasting pea | |
| Flowering pea of Arkansa. from Capt. Lewis | | |
| Lavatera Thuringica. | | |
| Lilly. The yellow of the Columbia. It's root a food of the natives. | | |
| Lobelia Cardinalis. | Scarlet Cardinal's flower. | |
| Lychnis Chalcedonica. | Scarlet Lychnis | |

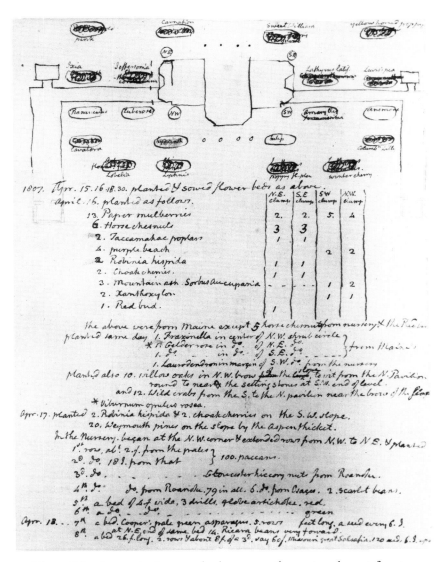

Plan of the flower beds near the house on the east and west fronts, drawn by Jefferson in the spring of 1807. (*Courtesy of the Historical Society of Pennsylvania*)

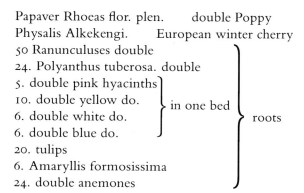

Papaver Rhoeas flor. plen.        double Poppy
Physalis Alkekengi.        European winter cherry
50 Ranunculuses double
24. Polyanthus tuberosa. double
5. double pink hyacinths
10. double yellow do.        } in one bed
6. double white do.
6. double blue do.
20. tulips                                        } roots
6. Amaryllis formosissima
24. double anemones

His granddaughter Ellen Randolph Coolidge wrote years later to Henry S. Randall, Jefferson's biographer:

> I remember well when he first returned to Monticello, how immediately he began to prepare new beds for his flowers. He had these beds laid off on the lawn, under the windows, and many a time I have run after him when he went out to direct the work, accompanied by one of his gardeners, generally Wormley, armed with spade and hoe, whilst he himself carried the measuring-line. I was too young to aid him, except in a small way, but my sister, Mrs. Bankhead, then a young and beautiful woman, . . . was his active and useful assistant. I remember the planting of the first hyacinths and tulips, and their subsequent growth. The roots arrived, labelled each one with a fancy name. There was Marcus Aurelius, and the King of the Gold Mine, the Roman Empress, and the Queen of the Amazons, Psyche, the God of Love, etc., etc., etc. Eagerly, and with childish delight, I studied this brilliant nomenclature, and wondered what strange and surprisingly beautiful creations I should see rising from the ground when spring returned, and these precious roots were committed to the earth under my grandfather's own eye, with his beautiful grand-daughter Anne standing by his side,

and a crowd of happy young faces, of younger grandchildren, clustering round to see the progress, and inquire anxiously the name of each separate deposit. Then, when spring returned, how eagerly we watched the first appearance of the shoots above ground. Each root was marked with its own name written on a bit of stick by its side, and what joy it was for one of us to discover the tender green breaking through the mould, and run to grandpapa to announce, that we really believed Marcus Aurelius was coming up, or the Queen of the Amazons was above ground! With how much pleasure compounded of our pleasure and his own, on the new birth, he would immediately go out to verify the fact, and praise us for our diligent watchfulness. Then, when the flowers were in bloom, and we were in ecstasies over the rich purple and crimson, or pure white, or delicate lilac, or pale yellow of the blossoms, how he would sympathize in our admiration, or discuss with my mother and elder sister new groupings and combinations and contrasts. Oh, these were happy moments for us and for him!

Jefferson left these "happy moments" for the drudgery of Washington official life on May 13. His mind was still on his gardens. He continually sent memoranda and instructions to his faithful overseer, Edmund Bacon. This one is typical of many he sent while president:

### Directions for Mr. Bacon

If the weather is not open and soft when Davy arrives, put the box of thorns into the cellar, where they may be entirely free from the influence of cold, until the weather becomes soft, when they must be planted in the places of those dead through the whole of the hedges which inclose the two orchards, so that the old and the new shall be complete, at 6 inches' distance from every plant. If any remain, plant them in the nursery of thorns. There are 2,000. I send Mr. Maine's written instructions about them, which must be followed most minutely. The other trees he brings are to be planted as follows:

4 Purple beaches. In the clumps which are in the southwest and northwest angles of the house, (which Wormley knows.) There were 4 of these trees planted last spring, 2 in each clump. They all died, but the places will be known by the remains of the trees, or by sticks marked No.IV. in the places. I wish these now sent to be planted in the same places.

4 Robinias, or red locusts. In the clumps in the N.E. and S.E. angles of the house. There were 2 of these planted last spring, to wit, 1 in each. They are dead, and two of them are to be planted in the same places, which may be found by the remains of the trees, or by sticks marked V. The other 2 may be planted in any vacant places in the S.W. and N.W. angles.

4 Prickly ash. In the S.W. angle of the house there was planted one of these trees last spring, and in the N.W. angle 2 others. They are dead. 3 of those now sent are to be planted in their places, which may be found by the remains of the trees, or by sticks marked VII. The fourth may be planted in some vacant space of the S.W. angle.

6 Spitzenberg apple trees. Plant them in the S.E. orchard, in any place where apples have been planted and are dead.

5 Peach trees. Plant in the S.E. orchard, wherever peach trees have died.

While Jefferson was president he visited Monticello at least twice each year, remaining there for several weeks at each visit. He rarely failed to bring with him plants and seeds to be grown in the nursery, the grove, the orchard, or the vegetable and flower gardens. Bacon recalled, "Mr. Jefferson sent home many kinds of trees and shrubbery from Washington.

I used to send a servant there with a great many fine things from Monticello for his table, and he would send back the cart loaded with shrubbery from a nursery near Georgetown that belonged to a man named Maine, and he would always send me directions what to do with it. He always knew all about everything in every part of his grounds and garden. He knew the name of every tree, and just where one was dead or missing."

Garden gossip continued between Jefferson and McMahon. On July 6, 1808, Jefferson wrote:

> Early in the next year I shall ask of you some cuttings of your bushes [gooseberries], and before that shall send a pretty copious list for a supply of the best kinds of garden seeds, and flowers. I shall be at home early in March for my permanent residence, and shall very much devote myself to my garden. . . . I have the tulips you sent me in great perfection, also the hyacinths, tuberoses, amaryllis, and the artichokes.

There was talk of various other flowers in the letters that followed. Jefferson's last letter to McMahon from Washington was on February 8, 1809, just a few days before he left for Monticello. Among the plants he asked to be sent him were crown imperials, lilies of the valley, and auriculas. He again remarked that his garden was going to occupy much of his attention when he got home. McMahon sent the plants ordered and also a collection of flower seeds.

Jefferson left the White House on March 11, 1809, and arrived at Monticello four days later. He began immediately to work with his flowers. A variety of plants had been sent by the nurseryman Main from Washington, and those he had ordered from McMahon were already there. The spring and summer of 1809 were busy seasons at Monticello. Planting continued in the fall. On November 6, the Garden Book recorded:

Planted from Mr. Lomax's
   3. Modesty shrubs, viz. 1. in N.E. circular bed, 1. in N.W. & 1. in S.W. do.
   5. Jujubes, viz. 1. in S.E. clump, 2. in S.W. do.   2. in N.W. do.
   21. Star jasmines. 2 in each of the oval beds
   24 Filberts in the lowest terras below the old filbert bush & every other one above includg. 7. terrasses.

During the spring of 1810, the interest and planting continued. McMahon continued to send plants. The Garden Book again recorded the plantings, which included:

Mar. 21. Planted 7. Rhododendrons in 4. oval beds in each corner of the house.
Apr. 18. Flower borders. Sowed larkspurs, poppies, balsam apple.
         N. oval bed on S.W. side. Nutmeg plant.
         S. oval bed on S.W. side. American Columbo.
   24. Planted 3. yellow
               Jasmines from    } in the oval beds next to the
               Mr. Coles        } covered ways on both sides
   25. 5. do. from Mr. Divers   } of each.

In addition to the many activities on the farm, the orchard, and the vegetable garden, there was much planting in the flower beds during the spring of 1811, including:

Mar. 22. Mimosa pudica. Sensitive plant. Oval bed in ∠ of N.W. Piazza & covered way.

Reseda odorata. Mignonette. Do. near N.W. cistern.

Delphinium exaltatum. American Larkspur. Outer flower border. N.W. quarter.

Pentapetes Phoenicia. Scarlet Mallow. Outer flower border. S.W. quarter.

23. Lathyrus odoratus. Sweet scented pea. Oval bed in S.W. ∠ of S.W. portico and do. S.W. ∠ of S. piazza and covd. way. Also Ximenesia Encelioides. In the same. Belle grande plante annuelle d'ornement. From Thouin

Apr. 8. Anemone pulsatilla. Belle plante vivace. Oval in S.W. ∠ of S.W. portico & chamber
Mirabilis tota varietas. Plante vivace d'ornement. Oval in N.W. ∠ of S.W. portico & Ding. R.

Apr. 16. Sowed seed of the silk plant from Mr. Erving in oval bed near the S.E. cistern.

Another letter from Jefferson to McMahon was sent on April 8, 1811:

> I have an extensive flower border, in which I am fond of placing *handsome* plants or *fragrant*. Those of mere curiosity I do not aim at, having too many other cares to bestow more than a moderate attention to them. In this I have placed the seeds you were so kind as to send me last. In it I have also growing the fine tulips, hyacinths, tuberoses & Amaryllis you formerly sent me. My wants there are Anemones, Auriculas, Ranunculus, Crown Imperials & Carnations . . . some handsome lillies. But the season is now too far advanced. During the next season they will be acceptable.

The "extensive flower borders" and the roundabout walk were laid out in the spring of 1808. Jefferson, however, had made definite plans for them in the spring of 1807. Narrow

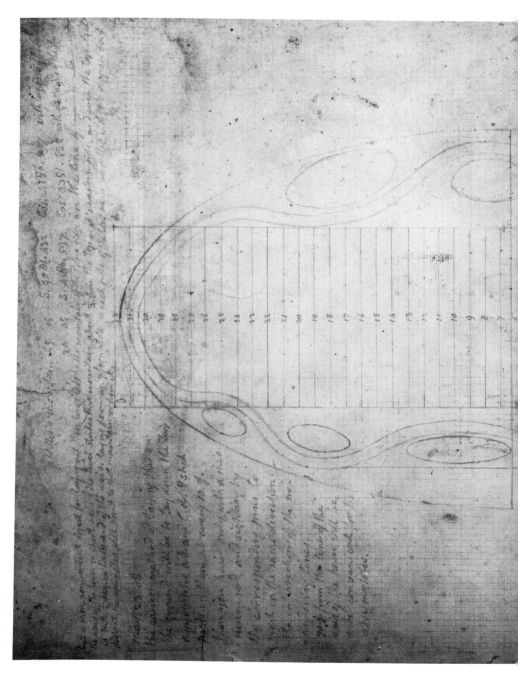

Plan of gravel roundabout walk on the west lawn drawn by Jefferson probably in the early 1790s, with notations on method of laying out the walk added in 1808. (*Courtesy of the Massachusetts Historical Society*)

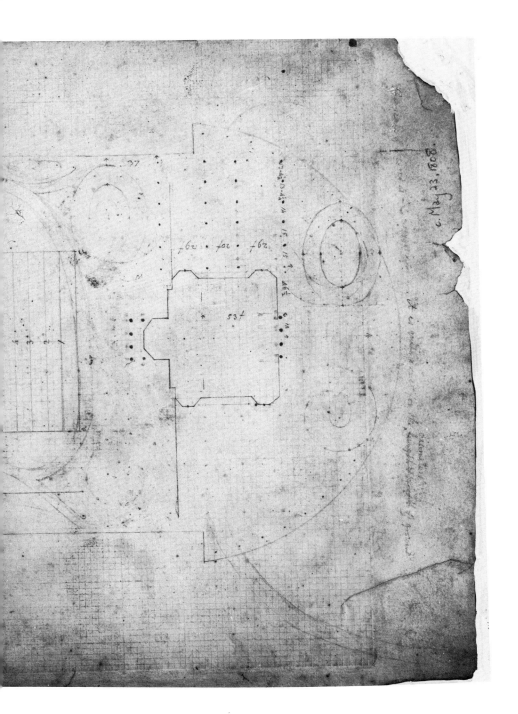

c. May 23, 1808.

flower borders were to outline the walk on both sides, and in the hollows of the walk oval beds for flowering shrubs were to be placed.

Jefferson had earlier made a drawing of the walk with oval beds for shrubs in the hollows of it. From this drawing he made a sketch on the back of a letter he sent in 1807 to his granddaughter Anne, who tended the flower garden at Monticello when he was away.

> Washington June 7. 07.
> My dear Anne
> . . . From yourself I may soon expect a report of your first visit to Monticello [she was then at her father's home, Edgehill], and of the state of our joint concerns there. I find that the limited number of our flower beds will too much restrain the variety of flowers in which we might wish to indulge, and therefore I have resumed an idea, which I had formerly entertained, but had laid by, of a winding walk surrounding the lawn before the house, with a narrow border of flowers on each side. This would give us abundant room for a great variety. I inclose you a sketch of my idea, where the dotted lines on each side of the black line shew the border on each side of the walk. The hollows of the walk would give room for oval beds of flowering shrubs.

This sketch showed several variations from the drawing. The contour of the walk was changed, the number of oval beds in the hollows of the walk was reduced from five to four, and their location was reversed.

Flower talk continued in letters that followed between Jefferson and his granddaughter, but no further mention was made of the flower borders and walks until the middle of February of the next year. In a letter to her he promised to lay out the borders around the level, on his first visit home.

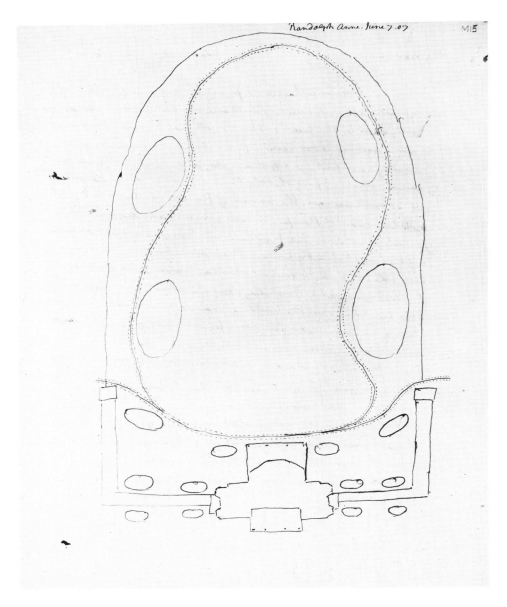

Plan of the gravel roundabout walk, borders, and beds sketched by Jefferson on the back of a letter to Anne Randolph on June 7, 1807. (*Courtesy of the Massachusetts Historical Society*)

Washington Feb. 16. 08.

My dearest Anne,

. . . I shall not attempt to get any more flower roots and seeds from Philadelphia this season, and must rely entirely on you to preserve those we have by having them planted in proper time. This you will see from McMahon's book, and Mr. Bacon will make Wormley prepare the beds whenever you let him know, so that they may be ready when you go over to set out the roots. The first time I come home I will lay out the projected flower borders round the level so that they shall be ready for the next fall; and in the spring of the next year I will bring home a full collection of roots and plants. We shall then have room enough for every thing.

Jefferson arrived at Monticello from Washington for his spring vacation of 1808 on May 11. He returned to Washington on June 8. During his vacation he laid out the winding walk and flower borders on the lawn before the house. He modified both the drawing and the sketch to fit better the contour of the lawn.

The borders were planted with a large variety of roots and seeds. Anne went to Port Royal in the fall of 1808, after her marriage to Charles Lewis Bankhead. She longed to see her grandfather and the flower border at Monticello. She wrote him on November 26:

On coming from Edgehill I left all the flowers in Ellens care, however I shall be with you early enough in march to assist about the border, which the old French Gentlemens [Thouin's] present [seeds] if you mean to plant them there, with the wild and bulbous rooted ones we have already, will compleatly fill.

The present reconstructed walk follows exactly the depression of the old walk in the ground. For years irises, tulips,

The twinleaf, or Jeffersonia (*Jeffersonia diphylla*), a shy, woodland wildflower, blooms in early April. It was named in Jefferson's honor by Benjamin S. Barton, a noted early American botanist, in 1792.

Jefferson planted the "Chinese Ixia" in an oval flower bed in 1807. This robust, summer-blooming perennial is now referred to as blackberry lily (*Belamcanda chinensis*).

When Jefferson planted the geranium, he was growing a plant only recently introduced into American gardens. These geraniums (*Pelargonium inquinans*) are the species, or wild, form of the plant as it grows in its native South Africa. Our modern race of bedding plants evolved, in part, from this species.

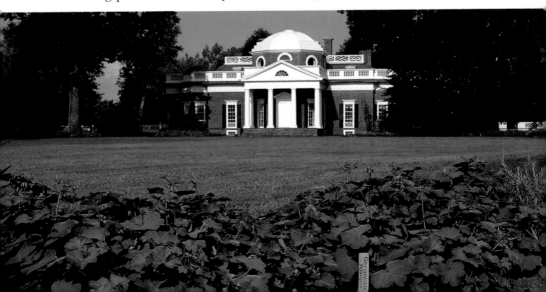

The roundabout flower walk, fishpond, and oval beds on the west front during late April.

The silverbell (*Halesia carolina*) in April.

Lavender (*Lavandula angustifolia*) with white clover.

Foxgloves (*Digitalis purpurea*) bloom in an oval bed on the east front during early June.

The roundabout walk in June is ornamented by lavender (*Lavandula angustifolia*), snapdragons (*Antirrhinum majus*), corn poppies (*Papaver rhoeas*), the species form of African marigold (*Tagetes erecta*), lilies (*Lilium regale*), and larkspur (*Consolida orientalis*).

White snapdragons (*Antirrhinum majus*), horminum sage (*Salvia viridis*), corn poppies (*Papaver rhoeas*), calendula (*Calendula officinalis*), larkspur (*Consolida orientalis*), opium poppies (*Papaver somniferum*), oriental poppies (*Papaver orientale*), African marigolds (*Tagetes erecta*), and cheeses mallow (*Malva sylvestris*) bloom along the roundabout flower walk near the North Pavilion.

Tulips (*Tulipa* sp.) bloom in an oval flower bed with yellow wall-flowers (*Cheiranthus cheiri*), the native red columbine (*Aquilegia canadensis*), and wood hyacinths (*Endymion hispanicus*).

jonquils, hyacinths, and other plants had come up in the spring on either side of the walk. These plants indicated the location of the borders and the walk which they outlined. Although the plan of 1807 showed continuous borders of flowers extending the entire length of the walk, in restoring them they were laid out only to the North and South Pavilions and broken at intervals to meet the conditions at Monticello today.

Mrs. Margaret Bayard Smith, who visited Jefferson in the summer of 1809, found that "the course round this back lawn was a qr. of a mile." Randall, Jefferson's biographer, wrote of the flower borders and gravel walk, "The flowers were mostly cultivated in plats and borders on the lawns. On the rear lawn, an elliptical gravel walk, 'the round-about walk', commenced at the portico and extended some distance outside of the space hemmed in by the buildings."

Many years after he left Virginia, Edmund Bacon, describing Monticello to the Reverend H. W. Pierson, gave further evidence of the location of the walks and borders, and of the loveliness of the grounds:

> The grounds around the house were most beautifully orna-
> mented with flowers and shrubbery. There were walks, and
> borders, and flowers, that I have never seen or heard of any-
> where else. Some of them were in bloom from early in the
> spring until late in the winter. A good many of them were
> foreign. Back of the house was a beautiful lawn of two or
> three acres, where his grandchildren used to play a great
> deal.

From 1808 through 1812, the flower borders outlining the gravel walk reached their perfection. On November 15, 1808, in a letter to his granddaughter Ellen, Jefferson wrote, "I have 700 species of seeds sent me by Mr. Thouin from the National garden of France." A large number of these were planted in the borders at Monticello. Ellen, reporting about the condition of the garden in December of the same year, wrote to Jefferson, "There are at least a peck of tuberose and 12 or 14 Amaryllys roots all packed in bran." They had been dug from the flower borders for winter storage. As late as 1816, Jefferson wrote to his daughter Martha from Poplar Forest, his other home, in Bedford County, Virginia, to send him some "of the hardy bulbous roots of flowers . . . Daffodils, jonquils, Narcissuses, flags and lillies of different kinds, refuse hyacinths" from the flower borders, to be planted at Poplar Forest. This request indicates that the flower bulbs had so increased at Monticello that there were enough to send elsewhere.

Several letters passed between Jefferson and McMahon during the month of February 1812. On the sixteenth, Jefferson ordered, among other items, seeds of auricula, double anemone, double carnation, mignonette; bulbs of crown imperial, double ranunculus; plants of Cape jasmine; and trees of cedar of Lebanon, balsam fir, cork oak, and European chestnut. McMahon sent the following plants on the twenty-eighth:

2 Roots Amaryllis Belladonna
6 pots of Auriculas, different kinds.
1 do. of a beautiful polyanthus
32 Roots best Tulips of Various kind
32 do. Best double Hyacinths assorted.
40 plants of the Hudson Strawberry . . .
4 roots Lilium superbum. L.
4 small plants Gooseberries, large red fruit & the best I have ever seen.
Some roots Amaryllis Atamasco L.

He also sent some grapevines and shrubs, including:

Symphoricarpos leucocarpa (mihi). This is a beautiful shrub brought by C. Lewis from the River Columbia, the flower is small but neat, the berries hang in large clusters are of a snow white colour and continue on the shrubs, retaining their beauty, all the winter; especially if kept in a Green House. The shrub is perfectly hardy; I have given it the trivial english name of Snowberry-bush.

Until 1812 Jefferson's flower borders were continuous, that is, the flowers were not arranged in groupings of definite sizes. On April 8 of this year the Garden Book recorded a new planting procedure:

> Flower borders. . . . Laid them off into compartmts. of 10.f length each.
>     in the N. borders are 43.  ⎫
>     in the S. borders are 44½  ⎬  comptmts.
>                                 ⎭
>     The odd compartments are for bulbs requirg. taking up
>     The even ones for seeds & permanent bulbs
>     Denote the inner borders. i. and the outer o.
> Sowed Bellflower in 28. on both sides   ⎫  There was by
>         African Marigold 32d. do.        ⎬  mistake an inter-
>         White poppy 42d. N. and 44th S.  ⎭  change of place
>                                             between one of
>                                             the parcels of
>                                             bellflower &
>                                             Poppy.

The year 1812 was a busy one among the flower beds and borders at Monticello. The mails brought new and interesting plants from McMahon. On September 16 came "3 roots of Crown Imperial which cary two tiers of flowers, *when in very luxuriant growth;* also 12 Roots of Gladiolus communis; both kinds hardy and fit for the open ground." On September 23 he sent "a small box containing 6 Dwarf Persian Iris, 12 Cloth of Gold Crocus, 6 Iris Xiphium *a new & fine variety,* 12

Double Persian Ranunculuses; with the seeds of some *very superior* Impatience Balsamina, Red Antwerp Raspberry & Centaurea macrocephala." On September 24 he sent: "3 Roots Antholiza aethiopica, a Green House bulb, 6 Feathered Hyacinth roots, Hyacinthus montrosus L. 3 Double blue Hyacinths, named *Alamode* by the Dutch, remarkably early & proper for forcing. 6 Roots of a beautiful variety of Crocus vernus, of very early bloom; flower white inside & beautifully striped outside. 2 Roots Parrot Tulips, color of the flowers red, green and yellow mixed. Some seed of the Mirabilis longiflora, or Sweet-scented Marvel of Peru." During the months of October, November, and December came more items, including: "6 Roots Watsonia Meriana," 12 roots of "Trittonia fenestrata," "6 Morea flexuosa," "1 Root silver striped Crown Imperial," "3 Roots *Amaryllis Belladonna,* or Belladonna Lily," and "some superior China Pink and Auricula seeds."

McMahon sent few plants to Jefferson after 1812, but their correspondence about garden matters continued for several years. The Garden Book is silent about flowers after this year, but letters to his granddaughters and friends give interesting glimpses of work among the flowers. There were also exchanges of plants with neighbors and friends in other parts of Virginia.

 *Planting is one of my great amusements, and even of those things which can only be for posterity, for a Septuagenary has no right to count on any thing beyond annuals.*

JEFFERSON TO DR. SAMUEL BROWN (1813)

# The Garden Restored

*Lunaria still in bloom. An indifferent flower.*
*Mirabilis just opened. Very clever.*
*Larger Poppy has vanished—Dwarf poppy still in bloom*
*but on the decline.*
*Carnations in full life.*
*Argemone, one flower out.*

NOTES FROM THE GARDEN BOOK

AS JEFFERSON grew older the care of the garden was gradually taken over by other members of the household. Mrs. Martha Jefferson Randolph, his daughter, carried most of the responsibility, with Wormley, the faithful gardener, doing much of the work. Jefferson wrote to Samuel Maverick, of South Carolina, on May 12, 1822, "Age, debility and decay of memory have for some time withdrawn me from attention to matters without doors." Despite these handicaps, he sent to Mrs. John Wayles Eppes in the same year:

> 2 trees of the most beautiful kinds known. The tallest is the
> *silk tree* from Asia. It will require housing about 2. years
> more and will then bear the open air safely. The mother tree
> growing here, about 15. years old and 25. f. high & still
> growing vigorously has stood winters which have killed my
> Azederacs & mulberries. The other is the celebrated *Bow
> wood* [Osage orange] of Louisiana which may be planted in

the spring where it is to stand as it bears our climate perfectly. It bears a fruit of the size and appearance of an orange, but not eatable.

This interest in gardening and plants continued until his death.

Jefferson died on July 4, 1826. A letter written on November 12 of the same year by his granddaughter Cornelia Randolph, from Monticello, to her sister Ellen, in Boston, gives us the names of some of the plants still growing at Monticello:

The day before yesterday a box was packed & despatched to you which when you open you will think contains a farrago from Morrissania, at least you will recognise our good aunt's blood in me. I was myself diverted at the temptation I experienced to be sending little remembrancers to you. First on the top of the box is a collection of trees for Mrs. Storer. I did not know what you had carried & lost, but thought I would make a collection according to my own taste; I chose then my favorite snowberry, so light & elegant in its form & foliage, and its berries so beautiful & pure, but most valued by me because it most flourishes when all other flowers have faded. The pyracantha which besides being very ornamental makes as you know a low hedge so thick that nothing can get through it. The yellow currant which for its fruit is of no value but it bears a quantity of beautiful yellow very fragrant flowers. The Halesia or snow drop tree which is so beautiful that I send it though I am afraid it will not bear the winter at fresh pond but it is worth trying. And the fringe tree which I know will not bear cold below zero, but as old madame Coolidge, I observed, cultivated green house plants, I thought I might send *her* this little acknowledgement of her kind attentions to me last summer, and in truth this tree is as well worthy a place in any green house as most of the most esteemed exotics. Nothing can be more beautiful than one particular plant that we have growing in our meadow here, behind a rock over which it bends & dips its long pendant graceful branches covered with fringe like flowers into the branch below; you know I love flowers and must excuse my dwelling so long on the beauties of one of the *prides* of our meadows & woods.

The charm and beauty of the garden at Monticello passed quickly after Jefferson's death. The house and grounds which had been Jefferson's dream for fifty years were sold to pay off his large debt. Curious people came in droves and carried away the choice plants, until there were few of them left. The lawn was later plowed up and planted with corn; the rare trees were cut down and replaced with mulberry trees to satisfy the craze for silkworm culture that was then sweeping the South.

A letter written by Virginia Randolph Trist, from Tufton, where she was then living, to Ellen Coolidge on March 23, 1827, gives a tragic picture of the changes going on at Monticello:

It will grieve you both very much to hear of the depredations that have been made at Monticello by the numerous parties who go to see the place. Mama's choicest flower roots have been carried off, one of her yellow jessamines, fig bushes (very few of which escaped the severe cold of last winter), grape vines and every thing and any thing that they fancied. N. [Nicholas Trist] consulted with Mr. Garrett and put a notice in the paper's requesting the visitors to desist from such tresspasses, but Burwell says that they have been worse *since* than they were before. As it appeared to be entirely useless to do any thing in that garden, Wormley is planting every thing down here.

Mrs. Margaret Bayard Smith made her second visit to Monticello in the summer of 1828. She gives a melancholy picture of the ruin that had set in there:

> How different did it seem from what it did 18 years ago! No kind friend with his gracious countenance stood in the Portico to welcome us, no train of domestics hastened with smiling alacrity to show us forward. All was silent. Ruin has already commenced its ravages—the inclosures, the terraces, the outer houses.

Monticello passed into other hands. The house barely escaped total ruin. Mrs. Smith's son, J. Bayard H. Smith, of Washington, who had visited Monticello when Jefferson was living there, went again in the summer of 1839. He wrote to his mother after the visit:

> My feelings upon reaching the summit of Monticello and entering the house, took me completely by surprise. I rode up the hill at a gallop without thought, but when I alighted and looked around me the associations of the place began to rush upon my mind and all were melancholy and sad. Around me I beheld nothing but ruin and change, rotting terraces, broken cabins, the lawn, ploughed up and cattle wandering among Italian mouldering vases, and the place seemed the true representation of the fallen fortunes of the great man and his family.

Desolation no longer hangs over Monticello. The Thomas Jefferson Memorial Foundation has brought back the old spirit of the place. Through the Garden Club of Virginia the flower garden has been restored. The serpentine roundabout walk, on the west lawn, where numbers of visitors had their morning and evening walks, and where they walked arm in arm with the great Jefferson himself, has been laid again. The oval and circular flower beds around the house, the flower borders along the gravel walk, have been restored and planted with the same kinds of flowers, shrubs, and trees that grew under the skilled protection of Jefferson.

In front of the house the gravel walk has been laid, and the semicircle of shrubs and weeping willows has been planted again. Posts and chains now enclose this semicircle of shrubs and trees as they did in Jefferson's time. The "setting stones," as Jefferson called them, are again on both sides of the lawn and afford resting places for tired visitors today as they did in his day. The fishpond reflects once more the beauties of the sky, the trees, and the house.

If Jefferson were living today he could write as he did in 1811 to his granddaughter Anne:

> The houses and the trees stand where they did. The flowers come forth like the belles of the day, have their short reign of beauty and splendor, and retire like them to the more interesting office of reproducing their like. The hyacinths and tulips are off the stage, the Irises are giving place to the Belladonnas, as this will to the Tuberoses . . .

 *I learn with great pleasure the success of your new gardens at Aulnay. No occupation can be more delightful or useful.*
JEFFERSON TO MADAME DE TESSÉ (1813)

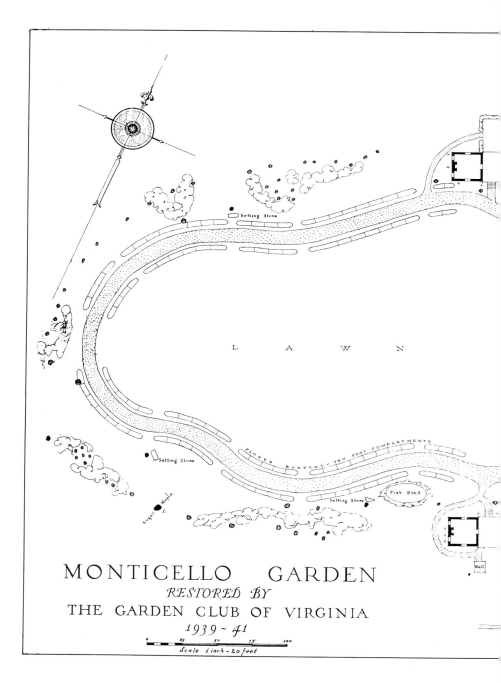

Setting Stone

L   A   W   N

FLOWER BORDERS—TEN FOOT COMPARTMENTS

Setting Stone

Sugar Maple

Setting Stone

Setting Stone    Fish Pond

Well

# MONTICELLO GARDEN
## *RESTORED BY*
## THE GARDEN CLUB OF VIRGINIA
### *1939 ~ 41*

0    25    50    75    100

*Scale 1 inch = 20 feet*

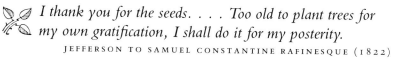 *I thank you for the seeds. . . . Too old to plant trees for my own gratification, I shall do it for my posterity.*

JEFFERSON TO SAMUEL CONSTANTINE RAFINESQUE (1822)

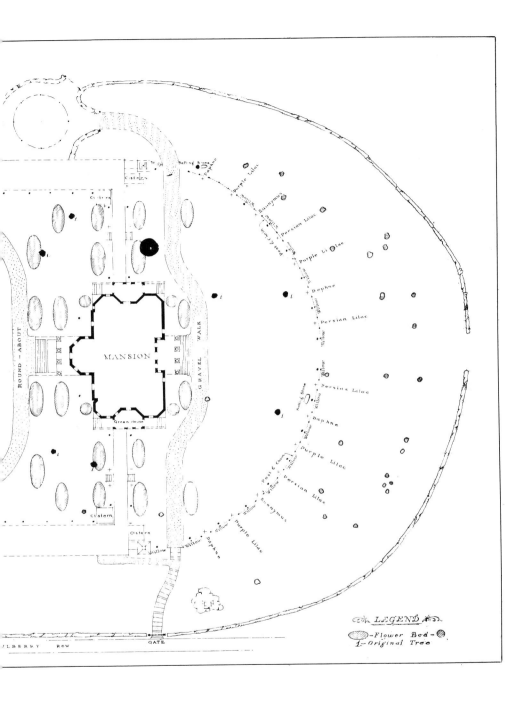

ROUND - ABOUT

MANSION

GRAVEL WALK

Green House

Cistern

Cistern

Cistern

GATE

MULBERRY ROW

Selling Stone
Daphne
Purple Lilac
Purple Lilac
Euonymus
Persian Lilac
Persian Lilac
Purple Lilac
Daphne
Willow
Persian Lilac
Willow
Willow
Persian Lilac
Willow
Selling Stone
Daphne
Willow
Purple Lilac
Willow
Post & Chain
Willow
Persian Lilac
Willow
Euonymus
Willow
Purple Lilac
Willow
Daphne
Willow

LEGEND

— Flower Bed —
1.- Original Tree

*And our own dear Monticello, where has nature spread so rich a mantle under the eye? mountains, forests, rocks, rivers. With what majesty do we there ride above the storms! How sublime to look down into the workhouse of nature, to see her clouds, hail, snow, rain, thunder, all fabricated at our feet! And the glorious Sun, when rising as if out of a distant water, just gilding the tops of the mountains, and giving life to all nature!*

JEFFERSON TO MARIA COSWAY (1786)

# An Annotated List of Flowers
# Grown by Thomas Jefferson

The following descriptive list of flowers grown by Jefferson includes the herbaceous annuals and perennials mentioned in the Garden Book, Weather Memorandum Book, letters, and memoranda of various sorts. The significance of his horticultural pursuits and the restored garden reside in this documentary wealth. It enables one not only to list the cultivated plants but to detail how and when a flower was grown by Jefferson and even, in some cases, how successful the planting was. There were two important gardening books in Jefferson's Monticello library; Bernard McMahon's *The American Gardener's Calendar,* 1806, and Philip Miller's *The Gardener's Dictionary,* which was published in London in 1768. Jefferson regularly consulted these classic works, and they are referred to often here because they illuminate the character and function of the flowers cultivated at Monticello.

The plants are arranged alphabetically according to their botanical genus. The common names follow with the specific names used by Jefferson delineated by quotation marks.

*Alcea rosea*   Hollyhock
Jefferson observed this centuries-old favorite flowering on June 10, 1767, and during June and July in his "Calendar of the bloom of flowers in 1782." The famous eighteenth-century English horticulturist Philip Miller, whose *Gardener's Dictionary* resided in the Monticello library, thought the hollyhock too ungainly for small flower gardens and recommended it be planted in "large wilderness borders or Avenues." Presently, hollyhocks are naturalized throughout the grounds at Monticello.

*Amaranthus hybridus* var. *erythrostachys*    Prince's-feather
Jefferson planted seeds of this summer-flowering annual on
April 4, 1767, at Shadwell and observed that it was similar to
a cockscomb (see *Celosia*). He noted "Amaranths" on an undated list of flowers, and it seems probable he grew two other
species of *Amaranthus* long cultivated in early American
flower gardens: *Amaranthus caudatus,* love-lies-bleeding, similar to the upright Prince's-feather but with drooping, bead-
like flowers, and possibly *Amaranthus tricolor,* Joseph's coat, a
brightly plumed foliage plant that Jefferson sent his brother-
in-law Francis Eppes from Paris in 1786.

*Amaryllis belladonna*    Belladonna lily
Bernard McMahon, Philadelphia nurseryman, author of *The
American Gardener's Calendar,* and Jefferson's gardening men-
tor, sent three bulbs to Monticello in 1812 and recommended
they be planted in a greenhouse "in pots of good rich mellow
earth; the flowers are beautiful and fragrant; their season of
flowering is Sept. & Oct." If Jefferson decided instead to plant
them outside, he might have followed the instructions in
McMahon's book of covering his amaryllis bed with three
inches of tanbark or "with mats laid on hoops, placed arch-
wise over them." McMahon also sent Jefferson two other
types of bulbs called "Amaryllis" by nineteenth-century gardeners: the Jacobean lily, *Sprekelia formosissima,* and the atamasco lily, *Zephyranthes atamasco,* native to the woodlands of
the southeast.

*Anemone coronaria* or *hortensis*    "Double anemone"
Jefferson ordered tubers of the "double Anemone" from Bernard McMahon in 1807. Both of the above species were
highly developed flowers by the beginning of the nineteenth
century, and there were numerous horticultural varieties offered in the nursery trade. In his book McMahon not only

provided "A Description of the Properties of a fine Double Anemone" but said the double varieties "being generally extremely beautiful, are particularly deserving of attention." The *Anemone coronaria,* poppy-flowered anemone, is still very popular.

*Anemone pulsatilla*    "Pasque flower"
This species of *Anemone,* a European wildflower, was sent to Monticello by André Thouin of the Jardin des Plantes in Paris. It was planted in an oval flower bed near the house in 1811. Jefferson also considered the pasqueflower suitable for naturalizing in 1771 when he listed the "hardy perennial flowers" for "the open ground on the west," an area he later called the Grove.

*Antirrhinum majus*    Snapdragon
This is another flower Jefferson thought suitable for naturalizing in 1771, and he observed it in bloom at Shadwell in 1767. The snapdragon is an excellent example of a flower whose appearance has changed little in three hundred years, although the recent development of miniature or dwarf varieties reflects the current interest in the Victorian practice of "bedding out" a carpet of color. Jefferson's snapdragon would have tended to be more ungainly than the Victorian or modern-day improved variety.

*Aquilegia canadensis*    Wild columbine
Thomas Mann Randolph, Jefferson's horticulturally astute son-in-law, observed this scarlet-flowering wildflower blooming on April 30, 1791, at Monticello. Jefferson also included "columbines" on an undated manuscript listing nu-

merous cultivated flowers, so it seems likely he grew the European columbine, *Aquilegia vulgaris*. This latter species, mentioned by McMahon in *The American Gardener's Calendar,* was the parent of many of the spur-type columbines grown today.

*Argemone mexicana*   Prickly poppy
Jefferson noted that "Argemone put out one flower" at Shadwell on June 18, 1767. A month later he remarked upon the appearance of another flower, "this is the 4th this year." Despite his wide-eyed vigilance it was hardly a successful season for this Mexican annual with pale yellow flowers and spiny, variegated foliage.

*Bellis perennis*   "Daisy"   English daisy
This is probably the "Daisy" Jefferson thought suitable for "the open ground on the west" in 1771. Although one can observe this species growing wild in English lawns, the hot, dry Virginia summer is an inhospitable host to this dainty biennial.

*Belamcanda chinensis*   "Chinese ixia"   Blackberry lily
Seeds of this oriental perennial, called "Chinese ixia" in the nineteenth century, were sent by McMahon and planted in an oval flower bed in 1807. Presently, this lilylike plant with its blackberry seeds and curious red-spotted orange flowers grows wild in central Virginia and at Monticello.

*Calendula officinalis*   "Marygold"   Calendula
When Jefferson planted the "Marygold" in 1767 he was referring to the pot marigold, or calendula, an annual grown for centuries as both a useful and ornamental plant. There is no

mention of the heat-loving *Tagetes,* the marigold so evident in today's summer garden, until 1808. Some of our popular tropical annuals had not been introduced by 1800, and many of the flowers brought early to American gardens, like the hardy calendula, were best suited to the cooler, moist summers of western Europe or at least the long Virginia spring.

*Campanula medium*   "Bellflower"   Canterbury bell
"Bellflower" was planted on both sides of the roundabout flower border in 1812. The biennial Canterbury bell, like the hollyhock and the sweet William, is typically associated with early American flower gardens.

*Celosia cristata*   Cockscomb
Jefferson noted the planting of "Cockscomb, a flower like the Prince's feather" in 1767. This is likely the crested form of *Celosia* with its strange, brainlike, scarlet combs. In 1811 Jefferson wrote McMahon: "I have an extensive flower border, in which I am fond of placing *handsome* plants or fragrant. Those of mere curiosity I do not aim at." Still, the cockscomb, like the sensitive plant, Venus flytrap, and others, would indeed qualify as a plant of "curiosity."

*Centaurea cyanus*   "French pink bleuette"   Cornflower
"French pink bleuette," "bluebottle" to the English and now known as cornflower or bachelor button, was among the cultivated flowers Jefferson listed on an undated manuscript. The pink-flowered form of this usually blue-blooming annual would, according to Philip Miller, be one of the variations "worthy of a Place in every good garden."

*Centaurea macrocephela*
This uncommon yellow-flowering, almost thistlelike perennial was sent to Monticello by Bernard McMahon in 1812. Nearly half the flower species cultivated at Monticello originated with this Philadelphia nurseryman.

*Chasmanthe aethiopica*
McMahon sent Jefferson "3 Roots Antholiza aethiopica, a Green House bulb" in 1812. This bright, summer-blooming flower is similar to a gladiolus and had just recently been introduced into American gardens from South Africa through the efforts of English plant explorers.

*Cheiranthus cheiri*   Wallflower
Jefferson requested the wallflower, an Old World biennial grown for centuries, especially in English gardens, from McMahon in 1807. In his book McMahon recommended the choicer, particularly the double-flowered, wallflowers be placed in pots and brought into the home or greenhouse for protection from the harsh American winter. Jefferson told his daughter Martha Randolph in 1806 that "Mrs. Nourse [a Washington friend] has just sent a bundle of Wall flowers for you . . . which I will ask Anne to take care of till March, when I will carry them to Monticello."

*Chimaphila maculata*   "Dragon's tongue"   Spotted wintergreen
This common wildflower, sometimes called pipsissewa, was noted as "Dragon's tongue" on an undated list of cultivated flowers. The spotted wintergreen, one of the first wildflowers learned by children, is conspicuous because of its variegated evergreen foliage and white summer flowers. The abundance of native plants transplanted from the Monticello woodlands

into the flower garden suggests it was as much a botanical collection, perhaps a laboratory for the study of local curiosities, as a showy display of colorful exotics.

*Consolida orientalis*   Larkspur
Jefferson sowed larkspur seed along the roundabout flower border in April 1810, noted it blooming at Shadwell in July 1767, and also thought it suitable for naturalizing in "the open ground on the west" in 1771. This is the hardy annual larkspur, an attractive relative of the majestic delphinium, which was not introduced until later in the nineteenth century.

*Convallaria majalis*   Lily of the valley
This spreading British native, "cultivated in Gardens for the Sweetness of the Flowers" according to Miller, now grows wild through much of Europe and around old homesteads in America. Jefferson thought it suitable for naturalizing in "the open ground on the west" in 1771 and ordered roots from McMahon in 1809. While other bulbous plants were taken up, divided, and replanted, a regular procedure for choice species, the lily of the valley was "to be left" as it is well suited to care for itself.

*Crocus angustifolia*   Cloth of gold crocus
Bernard McMahon sent twelve bulbs of this species, a Russian native popular in early English gardens, to Monticello in 1812.

*Crocus sativus*   Saffron crocus
Jefferson asked McMahon for "Saffron" in 1807. Although this crocus blooms in the fall and is less showy than the spring varieties, it is a plant of significant economic importance and has long been grown for the dried stigmas of the flower, used as a medicine, condiment, and dye.

*Crocus vernus*    Spring or Dutch crocus
This was another crocus from McMahon, who noted in 1812 that the variety he had sent was "of very early bloom; flowers white inside & beautifully striped outside."

*Cypripedium acaule*    "Mockaseen"    Pink lady slipper orchid
The English botanist John Bradbury visited Monticello in 1809 and remarked upon a number of unusual native plants, including three cypripedia, or lady slipper orchids. He noted that "some of these are removed into Mr. Jefferson's Garden and others are marked in the Woods & known to Col. R. [Randolph] who has this morning promised to take care of them for me." Jefferson also included the "Mockaseen," or moccasin flower, generally considered the rare and beautiful pink lady slipper, on his list of cultivated plants.

*Cypripedium calceolus* var. *pubescens*    Yellow lady slipper
Thomas Mann Randolph reported that this lovely orchid was blooming at Monticello on April 30, 1791. Although even less common than the pink lady slipper in Virginia woodlands, the yellow lady slipper is much more abundant in the Monticello forest and perhaps much more likely to have been transplanted into the flower garden. Today this would be considered a questionable practice, partly because increasing collection of rare native orchids threatens the species and also because most wild orchids suffer and usually die when removed from their native habitat.

*Delphinium exaltatum*    "American larkspur"
This unusual wild plant, sparsely scattered in the rich woods mostly along the Appalachian mountain chain, was planted

on the roundabout flower border in 1811. It is a coarse, shade-loving perennial with blue and purple flowers in late summer.

*Dianthus barbatus*    Sweet William
Jefferson noticed the "Sweet William begin to open" at Shadwell on April 16, 1767, reported flowers in May and June in 1782, and planted this biennial in an oval flower bed in 1807. Along with the roses, peonies, lilies, and iris, biennials such as the Canterbury bell and opium poppy, and the hardy annuals like the snapdragon, corn poppy, and larkspur, the flowering of the sweet William marked a peak of color in the garden during late spring.

*Dianthus caryophyllus*    Carnation
Seeds of the carnation, humbly called "gillyflower" despite the striped, multicolored improvements to the flower itself, were planted in one of the oval beds in April 1807. The unhappy fate of this important planting was relayed rather mercilessly to Jefferson by his granddaughter the following November: "The pinks Carnations Sweet Williams Yellow horned Poppy Ixia Jeffersonia everlasting Pea Lavatera Columbian Lilly Lobelia Lychnis double blossomed Poppy & Physalis failed, indeed none of the seeds which you got from Mr. McMahon came up."

*Dianthus chinensis*    "China pink," "Indian pink"
This was the third member of the genus planted in 1807 and, like the other two, has an intimate association with early American flower gardens. The "Indian pink" Jefferson planted at Shadwell in 1767 may have been this species or else *Dianthus plumarius,* the perennial cottage pink with its grasslike blue foliage.

*Dictamnus albus*   "Fraxinella"   Gas plant
Thomas Main, the Washington nurseryman, sent Jefferson a plant of this unusual perennial in 1807. It was planted in one of the "shrub circles" close to the house. The plant is named for the flash of ignited gas when a match is held close to the flower.

*Dionaea muscipula*   Venus flytrap
Jefferson requested seed of this unique insectivorous plant from David Ramsay of Charleston, South Carolina, in 1786, Benjamin Hawkins of Warrenton, North Carolina, in 1789 and 1796, William Hamilton of Philadelphia in 1800, and Timothy Bloodworth in 1804. He thanked Bloodworth for the seed: "It is the first I have ever been able to obtain, and shall take great care of it." Still, Jefferson's remarkable persistence seemed unrewarded as he was planting seed "several years old" in 1809. One wonders how successful he ever was with the Venus flytrap, a plant difficult to introduce into cultivation.

*Fritillaria imperialis*   Crown imperial lily
This spring-flowering bulb, long cherished for its dramatic orange tier of drooping bell-shaped flowers, was zealously requested of Bernard McMahon five times before the Philadelphia nurseryman shipped "3 roots . . . which carry two tiers of flowers, *when in very luxuriant growth.*" A month later he sent a variety with silver stripes. The bulbs evidently thrived at Monticello as Martha Randolph forwarded offshoots to Jefferson at Poplar Forest, his summer home, in 1816.

*Fritillaria pudica*   "Columbian lily"   Yellow fritillary
Bernard McMahon, curator of the Lewis and Clark plant collection, sent seeds of this Pacific Northwest native to

Monticello in 1807. When Jefferson planted it in an oval flower bed he remarked that "its root [was] a food of the natives." The yellow fritillary only grows to nine inches and has small purple-tinged yellow or orange flowers.

*Galanthus nivalis*   Snowdrop
Ellen Randolph wrote her grandfather in 1808 from Edgehill, a neighboring estate: "The third of April snow drops bloomed, you have none but I will give you mine if you want them, and have them set out in your garden when we go to Monticello." April 3 is very late for this white-blooming bulb, often the first flower of the season, and it seems possible that Ellen's "snow drops" were instead what we now call "snowflake," *Leucojum* sp.

*Gladiolus communis*   Gladiolus
Twelve bulbs of gladiolus, "hardy and fit for the open ground," were sent by Bernard McMahon in 1812. This purple-flowering European native is far removed from to-day's florist gladiolus, which is the result of intense hybridization beginning in the 1830s. John Parkinson, the noted English horticulturist of the seventeenth century, complained of the *Gladiolus communis* in his famous work, *Paradisi in Sole Paradisus Terristris (A Garden of Pleasant Flowers):* "If it be suffered any long time in a Garden, it will rather choak and pester it, than be an ornament unto it."

*Glaucium flavum*   Yellow-horned poppy
Seeds of this curious, sparse-flowering biennial were planted in an oval bed southeast of the house in 1807. This European native was introduced very early into American gardens and was even naturalized in Massachusetts as early as the seventeenth century.

*Gomphrena globosa*    Globe amaranth
Jefferson planted seeds of this summer-flowering annual in
1767 at Shadwell. A native of India, the globe amaranth has
been forever cultivated for its long-lasting flowers. At Monticello it was one of a limited number of heat-loving annuals
suitable for the long Virginia summer.

*Helianthus annuus* or *divaricatus*    Sunflower
When Jefferson listed the "Sunflower" among his "hardy perennial flowers" suitable for "the open ground on the west" in
1771, he was probably referring to the North American annual, which can reseed itself and serve as a perennial. It could
also be the perennial native to Monticello, *Helianthus divaricatus,* still abundant in the Grove to the west of the house.

*Heliotropium arborescens*    Heliotrope
Jefferson sent a number of plants to Francis Eppes from Paris
in 1786, including the lovely blue-flowering heliotrope: "To
be sowed in spring. A delicious flower, but I suspect it must
be planted in boxes & kept in the house in the winter. The
smell rewards the care."

*Hexaglottis longifolia*
This is an irislike, tender bulb, formerly called *Moraea flexu-
losa,* sent by McMahon in 1812 and probably planted in the
greenhouse. It has yellow flowers in May and had just recently been introduced from South Africa.

*Hyacinthus orientalis*    Hyacinth
Jefferson opened his *Garden Book* on March 30, 1766, with
the remark, "Purple hyacinth begins to bloom," and by his
return to Monticello from the presidency the hyacinth was
one of the more prominent flowers in the garden. Bernard

McMahon made four shipments of hyacinth bulbs between 1807 and 1812, when he wrote that "they are of the first rate kinds, and nearly of as many varieties as roots." Jefferson planted an oval bed with four different colors of double hyacinths in 1807, probably following the checkered planting plan sketched by McMahon in his book. His granddaughter described them the following spring when in flower as "superb ones." So successful was this early and fragrant flower that excess bulbs were forwarded from Monticello to Poplar Forest in 1816.

*Hypoxis hirsuta*   Yellow stargrass
"A little yellow flower from the woods Star of Bethlehem" was among the cultivated flowers listed on an undated memorandum. Although Philip Miller described it as "a very humble Plant," he still reserved precious space for it in his London greenhouse so that it would flower throughout the cooler English summer and produce seed.

*Impatiens balsamina*   Balsam
"Double balsam" was planted at Shadwell in April 1767 and ordered from Bernard McMahon in 1812. This was among the "more valuable and curious sorts of tender annuals" to McMahon, who gave detailed instructions for the raising of young plants in hot beds, which were cold frames heated by decomposing manure. Balsams, especially the newly developed double varieties with striped flowers, were more esteemed in Jefferson's time than they are today.

*Ipomoea quamoclit*   Cypress vine
Jefferson forwarded seeds of this tender annual vine to his two daughters, Mary and Martha, in 1791 from Philadelphia. The seeds were planted "in boxes in the window," probably

to serve as houseplants, at Monticello the following March. In 1808 Anne Cary Randolph noted in a letter to her grandfather that Mrs. Nicholas Lewis, a neighbor and active gardener, had saved more seed for him of this morning glory relative with star-shaped, scarlet flowers.

*Iris germanica*   "Flag"   German or Bearded iris
This species is the common flag, an integral though seldom-mentioned flower of the late spring border, the indestructible "iris" Jefferson found suitable for naturalizing in 1771, and for Philip Miller, appropriate "only for large Gardens, or to plant in Wilderness-quarters." The "Iris bicolor" observed in the 1782 flower calendar may be a variety of this species.

*Iris persica*   "Dwarf Persian iris"
Six bulbs of this unusual species were sent by McMahon in 1812. A native of Iran and Turkey with greenish-blue flowers and a yellow keel, the Persian iris has a reputation of being difficult to grow. McMahon, however, found it most suitable for forcing in February with the aid of a greenhouse or hot bed.

*Iris pseudoacorus*   "Flower-de-luces"   Yellow iris
In a May 28, 1767, notation in his Garden Book, Jefferson said "Flower-de-luces just opening." This is the yellow-flowering fleur-de-lis of history, native to western Europe, and now naturalized in wet soils in northern America. It was so common about the English landscape that Miller said it was "seldom admitted into Gardens."

*Iris xiphium*    Spanish iris
McMahon also sent this species to Jefferson in 1812 and described it as *"a new & fine variety."* This is a parent of the Dutch iris so popular today and a good example of one of the many newly introduced species relayed by McMahon to Monticello.

*Jeffersonia diphylla*    Jeffersonia, Twinleaf
Named for Jefferson by Benjamin S. Barton, a noted early American botanist, before a meeting of the American Philosophical Society in 1792, it was planted in one of the oval beds in 1807. This shy, woodland wildflower resembles a bloodroot in bloom, flowers near the time of Jefferson's early April birthday, and is perhaps most remarkable for its deeply cut, indented leaves, which inspired the common name, "twinleaf."

*Lathyrus latifolius*    Everlasting pea
This perennial pink-flowered sweet pea was among "the hardy perennial flowers" in 1771 and was also planted in an oval bed in 1807. Like many of the favorite flowers in early American gardens, the everlasting pea is now naturalized throughout the eastern United States along roads and at the edge of fields. However, it is now somewhat neglected in gardens despite its persistent summer-blooming flowers.

*Lathyrus odoratus*    Sweet pea
Jefferson planted seeds obtained from André Thouin of Paris in two of his oval beds in 1811. The sweet pea is another flower associated with old, particularly English, gardens, and

it does thrive in the cool, moist summers of western Europe. Still, it was popular enough in this country that Bernard McMahon listed five varieties in *The American Gardener's Calendar.*

*Lavatera olbia*   "The shrub marshmallow"   Tree lavatera
Seeds of this short-lived shrub, considered a herbaceous perennial by many, were planted in the Monticello nursery, which was at southeastern end of the vegetable garden. They were sent in 1807 by Doctor Gouan of Montpelier, France, and, if ever transferred to an oval bed, would have provided a striking display with their hollyhocklike purple flowers during midsummer. The tree lavatera is a plant native to the Mediterranean and is as rarely cultivated in America now as it was in Jefferson's day.

*Lavatera thuringiaca*
This was another unusual mallowlike perennial planted in an oval bed in 1807. It is a European native with purplish-pink flowers. See *Dianthus caryophyllus* for the unhappy fate of this planting.

*Lilium canadense*   "Canada martagon"   Canadian lily
While in Paris in 1786 Jefferson wrote home to his gardener, Anthony Giannini, and requested that a number of seeds, bulbs, and plants be forwarded overseas. The list included the "Lily of Canada. This is the lily which George [a trusted slave] found for me in the woods near the stone spring. I think that before I left home we took up some roots and planted them in the flower borders near the house." Although no plan for these early "flower borders" survive, this handsome native lily evidently thrived, and in 1809 Jefferson was exchanging bulbs with neighbors.

*Lilium candidum*    "White lilly"    Madonna lily
When Jefferson observed the "White Lilly" flowering in late
May 1782 he was referring to the ancient Madonna lily, introduced into the New World by the Pilgrims and one of the
oldest cultivated flowers known. It was so common in
eighteenth-century England that Philip Miller thought it "so
well known, that it will be needless to say any thing of it."

*Lilium chalcedonicum*    "Fiery" lily    Scarlet turk's-cap lily
This is probably the "Fiery" lily Jefferson noted blooming in
late May in "a Calendar of the bloom of flowers in 1782."
The scarlet turk's cap is a native of Greece, prominently listed
in McMahon's *Calendar,* and somehow absent from modern
American gardens.

*Lilium superbum*    "Alleghany martagon"    Turk's-cap lily
In 1809 Jefferson wrote to Judge William Fleming, a lifelong
friend in Richmond, and thanked him for sending the foliage
of the "Alleghany Martagon . . . A plant of so much beauty
& fragrance will be a valuable addition to our flower gardens.
Should you find your roots of it I shall be very thankful to
participate of them, & will carefully return you a new stock
should my part succeed & yours fail." Jefferson also ordered
this stately native lily with its reddish-orange flowers from
McMahon in 1812.

*Lobelia cardinalis*    Cardinal flower
Jefferson planted this brilliant summer-blooming wildflower
in an oval bed in 1807. Although the seed he planted came
from Bernard McMahon in Philadelphia, the cardinal flower
grows along streams on the lower parts of Monticello Mountain. It was in McMahon's book that American gardeners
were first urged to search the local woodlands and fields for

"the various beautiful ornaments with which nature has so profusely decorated them." Wildflowers are particularly suited for the mid and late summer when American gardens "are almost destitute of bloom" while the nearby meadow can be a waving tapestry of color. "Is it because they are indigenous that we should reject them?" asked McMahon. "What can be more beautiful than our Lobelias, Orchis, Asclepias, and Asters . . . ?"

*Lunaria annua*   Honesty or Money plant
On April 25, 1767, Jefferson noted in his Garden Book, "Lunaria still in bloom. an indifferent flower." The money plant is generally grown, not for its small purple flowers, but for its coin-shaped, silvery seed pods, which provide a lasting adornment to the summer border.

*Lupinus subcarnosus* or *texensis*   "Lewis' pea," "Arkansas pea"   Texas bluebonnet
Bernard McMahon, caretaker for the initial collection of plants brought east by the Lewis and Clark expedition, sent seeds of "the flowering Pea of the plains of Arkansas, a Lupinus," probably *L. subcarnosus* or Texas bluebonnet, to Monticello in 1807. Jefferson subsequently planted it in an oval bed and in later years even sowed seeds in the vegetable garden, promoting the soil-enriching qualities of this bright-flowered legume.

*Lychnis chalcedonica*   "Scarlet lychnis"   Maltese cross
This June-blooming perennial, grown for centuries in Europe and still popular today, was planted in an oval flower bed in 1807. When Jefferson noted the "Lychnis bloom" in 1767 at Shadwell he was possibly referring to the woolly-leaved rose campion, *Lychnis coronaria,* also very popular in early American gardens.

*Malva sylvestris*   "French mallow"
Jefferson grew numerous mallow-type flowers, including the common hollyhock, the marshmallow (*Althaea officinalis*), a medicinal herb, two species of *Lavatera* in 1811, the "Scarlet Mallow" (*Pentapetes phoenicia*) also in 1811, and the "Eastern mallow" (unidentified) in 1767. He also noted on an undated list of cultivated flowers the "French mallow," which is probably *Malva sylvestris,* a European native with purplish-pink flowers.

*Matthiola incana*   "Gilliflower"   Stock
This is likely the "Gilliflower" Jefferson found suitable for naturalizing in "the open ground on the west" in 1771, although the garden carnation was also called by this name. It would be extremely difficult to naturalize either flower because of the freezing winters and hot, dry summers at Monticello.

*Mertensia virginica*   "Mountain cowslip"   Virginia bluebell
One of the first notations in his Garden Book was on April 16, 1766, when Jefferson observed "a bluish colored, funnel-formed flower in low-grounds in bloom." He later introduced this wildflower into the flower border where its striking blue flowers would have blended handsomely with the narcissi, hyacinths, and tulips of early spring.

*Mesembryanthemum crystallinum*   Ice plant
Jefferson forwarded seeds of this tender annual from Washington to his granddaughter Anne in 1808, and they were later planted in a pot in the house. The succulent ice plant is distinguished by its sharply glistening foliage, a sprawling growth habit, and bright flowers that only open to the sun. Surely, it qualifies as another of Jefferson's flowers of "curiosity."

*Mimosa pudica*   Sensitive plant

Still another "curiosity." Seeds of the sensitive plant, a tender annual with pink, mimosalike flowers, were planted at Shadwell in 1767 and in a Monticello oval bed in 1811. Seeds for the latter planting were sent by Bernard McMahon, who uncharacteristically describes the plant in his book: "The sensibility of this plant is worthy of admiration, that with the least touch, or concussion of air, the leaves just like a tree a dying, droop and complicate themselves immediately, and presently after recover, resuming their former position; so that a person would be induced to think they were really endowed with this sense of feeling."

*Mirabilis jalapa*   Four-o'clock

In July 1767 Jefferson observed his four-o'clocks, "Mirabilis just opened very clever," and in 1811 he noted planting seed in one of his oval beds and remarked, "Mirabilis tota varietas, plante vivace d'ornement." The seeds were sent by André Thouin of the Jardin des Plantes in Paris. Early gardeners would marvel over the ability of this fanciful period plant, now fallen from favor with modern gardeners, not only to produce multicolored flowers on an individual specimen but to display its open flowers only at the approach of evening.

*Mirabilis longiflora*

Seeds of this species, a sweet-scented version of the common four-o'clock, were sent by McMahon in 1812. It has long, white tubular flowers and is indigenous to the American southwest.

*Momordica balsamina*   Balsam apple

This tender annual vine was planted along the roundabout flower border in the spring of 1812. The balsam apple's

Jefferson planted four-o'clocks (*Mirabilis jalapa*), "plante vivace d'ornement," in an oval flower bed near the house in 1811. (Photo by Andy Johnson)

Overleaf: Along the roundabout walk in summer snapdragons, spiderflowers (*Cleome hasslerana*), statice (*Limonium sinuatum*), strawflowers (*Helichrysum bracteatum*), and New England asters (*Aster novaeangliae*) are in bloom. (Photo by Robert Llewellyn)

Flowers of the sweet-scented mignonette (*Reseda odorata*). Jefferson wrote Bernard McMahon in 1811: "I have an extensive flower border, in which I am fond of placing *handsome* plants or fragrant. Those of mere curiosity I do not aim at." (Photo by Peggy Newcomb)

The cockscomb (*Celosia cristata*), a "curiosity" of the summer border.

Jefferson said the heliotrope (*Heliotropium arborescens*) was "a delicious flower. . . . The smell rewards the care."

Opium poppy (*Papaver somniferum*). (Photo by Peggy Newcomb)

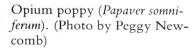

glossy, delicate foliage, small yellow flowers, and bursting orangish-red fruits were another novel addition to the summer border.

*Muscari comosum* var. *monstrosum*   Feathered hyacinth
Jefferson noted in his Garden Book that the feathered hyacinth bloomed on April 25, 1767, at Shadwell and throughout late May and into June in 1782. Bernard McMahon also forwarded bulbs in 1812. This late-flowering hyacinth with shredded blue flowers is now naturalized throughout the grounds at Monticello.

*Narcissus* sp.   Daffodil, Jonquil
When Jefferson asked his daughter Martha Randolph to send "daffodils, jonquils, Narcissuses" to him at Poplar Forest in 1816, he was probably just requesting various varieties and species of *Narcissus,* commonly called daffodil. Jefferson's jonquil could be *N. jonquilla* or simply any daffodil with a shallow cup or crown. He dug his daffodils after they bloomed and replanted them in October, a questionable practice for a flower so easily left alone. The uncommon reliance upon perennial bulbs at Monticello insured a persistent garden with low maintenance requirements—ideal for a gardener like Jefferson, who was absent for extended periods and who often had more practical landscape improvements in mind.

*Nigella sativa*   "Nutmeg plant"   Nigella
Jefferson planted this hardy annual in an oval flower bed on April 18, 1810. Although the seeds are used as a seasoning, the nutmeg plant's blue flowers, delicate, lacy foliage, and inflated seed pods make it a handsome ornamental as well.

*Paeonia officinalis*    Peony
This is the European species, one of the parents of our modern varieties, that Jefferson thought suitable for naturalizing in 1771. In the "Calendar of the bloom of flowers in 1782" Jefferson observed peonies in flower from mid-June through September, a rather incredible stretch for a flower which usually only lasts two weeks in late May and June.

*Papaver rhoeas*    "Dwarf poppy," "Lesser poppy"    Corn poppy
Jefferson planted "Papaver Rhoeas flor. plen. double poppy" in an oval bed in 1807. This is a horticultural variety of the common European field poppy, which was immortalized in Flanders during World War I. This is probably the "dwarf" or "lesser" poppy Jefferson observed blooming at Shadwell in 1767 and perhaps the "poppy" he found suitable for naturalizing in the Grove in 1771.

*Papaver somniferum*    "White poppy," "Larger    poppy"
Opium poppy
The "White poppy," a garden variety of opium poppy, was planted along the roundabout flower border in April 1812. This was one of the numerous hardy annuals to grace the flower gardens in late May and early June before the heat of high summer. Philip Miller said, "There are few plants whose flowers are so handsome, but having an offensive scent and being of short duration, they are not much regarded."

*Pelargonium inquinans* or *zonale*    Geranium
Jefferson grew the geranium, a recent South African introduction, as a houseplant both at the President's House in Washington (now the White House) and at Monticello. As he was about to leave the presidency, Margaret Bayard Smith, a

friend and prominent Washington socialite, asked him for a geranium that was growing in a windowed cabinet. Demonstrating the affinity of plants and man, gardening and sociability, Jefferson replied: "It is in very bad condition, having been neglected latterly, as not intended to be removed. He cannot give it his parting blessing more effectually than by consigning it to the nourishing hand of Mrs. Smith. If plants have sensibility, as the analogy of their organisation with ours seems to indicate, it cannot but be proudly sensible of her fostering attentions. Of his regrets at parting with the society of Washington, a very sensible portion attaches to Mrs. Smith, whose friendship he has particularly valued."

*Pentapetes phoenicia*   "Scarlet mallow"
Jefferson planted seeds of this plant, which were sent by McMahon, along the roundabout flower border in 1811. It is a tender annual from Asia with red flowers which open at noon and close at dawn. The "Scarlet Mallow" is rare in European gardens today and virtually unknown in America.

*Physalis alkekengi*   "European winter cherry"   Chinese lantern
Jefferson planted seeds of this European native in an oval flower bed in 1807. The ornamental seed pods, which appear late in summer, were once regarded as an edible fruit of some medicinal value.

*Podophyllum peltatum*   Mayapple
The mayapple was noted on an undated list of cultivated flowers. A prominent spring-blooming wildflower in the woodlands of Monticello, it was another in Jefferson's collection of native botanical curiosities. Margaret Bayard Smith described his plans for the grounds of the President's House

in *The First Forty Years of Washington Society:* "It was Mr. Jefferson's design to have planted them exclusively with Trees, shrubs and flowers indigenous to our native soil. He had a long list made out in which they were arranged according to their forms and colours and the seasons in which they flourished."

*Polianthes tuberosa*    Tuberose
Bernard McMahon sent double tuberoses to Monticello in 1807; they flowered on August 12; and on November 9 Anne Cary Randolph, after digging the roots, reported that "we shall have a plenty of them for the next year." As with the mignonette, the heliotrope, even trees like the wild crabapple, the tuberose was probably grown for the almost cloying sweetness of its flowers. Fragrant flowers were obviously a feature much appreciated in the more vivid atmosphere of early Virginia plantations.

*Primula auricula*    Auricula
McMahon sent "6 pots of Auriculas, different kinds" to Monticello in 1812. The garden auricula was much improved over its wild Swiss ancestor and much admired by the author of *The American Gardener's Calendar,* which includes detailed descriptions of the character and culture of what was considered a choice pot plant. McMahon gave directions for displaying the plants on greenhouse shelves, the proper compost including "one twenty-fourth ashes of burned vegetables," and devoted an entire page to the "Properties of a fine Variegated Auricula."

*Primula × polyantha*    Polyanthus
McMahon also sent "a beautiful polyanthus" in 1812. The polyanthus was another choice improved early nineteenth-century flower and was the result of the cross between the

English primrose (*Primula vulgaris*) and a red form of the English cowslip (*Primula veris*). McMahon's directions for the culture of the polyanthus were as detailed as for the auricula, and there was much interest in displaying the most fanciful colored flowers in pots. There is not as much interest in primulas presently in the United States, perhaps because they suffer during the long, hot summer.

*Primula vulgaris*   Primrose

When Jefferson listed the primrose among the "hardy perennial flowers" suitable for naturalizing in 1771, he was likely referring to this yellow-flowering native of the English woodland. Philip Miller in *The Gardener's Dictionary* said that "if they are placed under [a] hedge, and in shady Walks, they make a beautiful Appearance early in the Spring, when few other Plants are in Flower."

*Ranunculus asiaticus*   Persian buttercup

Like the other bulbs planted in the 1807 oval bed scheme, the ranunculuses were at least immediately successful. However, by 1812 Jefferson ordered more from Bernard McMahon, which suggests that perhaps these tender bulbs were not lifted and stored during the freezing winter months. Presently, the ranunculus is generally neglected in gardens, although it is a much-admired florist's flower.

*Reseda odorata*   Mignonette

Anne Cary Randolph wrote to her grandfather in 1803 that "we were so unfortunate as to lose the Mignonett entirely although Mama divided it between Mrs. Lewis Aunt Jane & herself but none of it seeded." Jefferson would plant this extremely fragrant annual in an oval bed in 1811, yet he included it among the seeds "which I do not now possess" in a letter to McMahon the following year. Surely the mignonette would be among those plants whose "smell rewards the care."

*Saponaria officinalis*   "Soapwort"   Bouncing Bet
This robust perennial was listed on an undated manuscript of cultivated flowers. Philip Miller said it was "a plant of no great Beauty; and, being a very great Runner in Gardens, has been almost excluded from all curious Gardens; but as it is a Plant which requires very little Culture, it may be admitted to have a Place in some abject Part of the Garden." The soapwort, like the daylily, perennial pea, and other aggressive early introductions into American flower gardens, is a common escape from cultivation today.

*Sisyrinchium angustifolium*   Blue-eyed grass
Jefferson included "a little bleu flower from woods Bermudian" on a list of cultivated flowers. Although this delicate blue flower is not usually cultivated, it would be a colorful and sensible addition to Monticello's wildflower collection.

*Solanum pseudocapsicum*   Jerusalem cherry
Ellen Randolph wrote her grandfather in 1808: "I have got the seed of the Jerusalem Cherry which I am told is very beautiful." Presently this tender plant is generally regarded as a cheery houseplant with its showy red berries. However, as a garden curiosity it would have been harmonious with the other novelties of the summer border at Monticello.

*Sprekelia formosissima*   Jacobean lily
Bernard McMahon sent six bulbs of the "Amaryllis formosissima" to Monticello in 1807. They were planted in an oval bed in the southwest angle of the house. The flower of this tender bulb can be compared to a stunning, scarlet insect,

even the flower of the bird-of-paradise, and was described by McMahon as "very admirable," "of extraordinary beauty," "and making a most beautiful and grand appearance."

*Swertia caroliniensis*   "American columbo"
This rare woodland perennial was planted in an oval flower bed in 1810. Peter Collinson, an early English botanist and sponsor of plant explorer John Bartram, described this plant as the "pyramid of Eden" because of its stately two-foot panicle of purple-spotted yellowish-white flowers.

*Tagetes erecta*   African marigold
Jefferson sowed the seed of the African marigold, a relatively recent import from South America, along the roundabout flower border on April 8, 1810. Bernard McMahon offered both the double and quilled forms now taken for granted, but which were developed from the wild species form with single flowers. Anne Cary Randolph wrote her grandfather in 1808 that "we have plenty of the two kinds of Marigolds that you gave us." This may suggest the French marigold, *Tagetes patula,* was also being grown at Monticello.

*Tritonia hyalina*   This South African bulb with bright yellow flowers was sent by McMahon in 1812. Many plant explorers were engaged to collect South African plants for Kew Gardens in London during the late eighteenth century, and it seems likely McMahon was the chief American curator for this collection.

*Trollius europaeus*   Globeflower
Jefferson included this European perennial among the "hardy perennial flowers" suitable for the "open ground on the west" in 1771. It would be difficult to naturalize this spring-blooming yellow flower at Monticello because of its need for moist, shady growing conditions.

*Tropaeolum majus*   Nasturtium
Although this bright-flowering tropical annual was planted yearly in the Monticello vegetable garden, it seems likely to have been included in the ornamental schemes as well. The peppery young leaves are eaten as a salad, the unexpanded flower buds are used as a garnish, and the seeds can be pickled for capers or as an aromatic seasoning.

*Tulipa* sp.   Tulip
The tulip was probably the most prominent and successful flower in the garden at Monticello. Bernard McMahon regularly sent the "best Tulips of Various kinds" including the spectacular parrot type, and he instructed they be "planted as directed on Page 528 of my book." The bulbs at Monticello were dug following their flowering, stored, then divided and replanted in the fall. In a letter to her grandfather in 1808 Anne Cary Randolph's lament strikes a common chord among tulip planters: "neither the hyacinths nor Tulips grow as regularly this spring as they did the last. Wormley [the gardener] in taking them up left some small roots in the ground which have come up about in the bed & not in the rows with the others." Many of the varieties grown at Monticello had the striped flowers that were fashionable then, rather than the solid colors so prominent in today's gardens.

*Verbesina encelioides*   "Ximenesia Encelioides"   Golden crownbeard
André Thouin of the Jardin des Plantes sent seeds of this Mexican annual to Monticello where it was planted in an oval bed in 1811. Thouin described it as a "belle grande plante annuelle d'ornement." Although most of the seeds sent from Paris were relayed by Jefferson to American botanical gardens

and plantsmen such as McMahon and William Hamilton, one laments that so few of these species were documented as actually planted at Monticello.

*Viola* sp.   "Dutch violet"   Violet
A few years after her grandfather's death, Cornelia Randolph sketched a floor plan of Monticello which included "violet beds" immediately outside the conservatory. Her sister Anne wrote Jefferson in 1808 and included a bouquet of fragrant white violets, perhaps from this same bed. The "Dutch violet," perhaps *V. odorata,* the wild white violet of Europe, was planted at Shadwell in 1767. *Viola canadensis* and *V. blanda* are two other native species of white violets possibly among "the hardy perennial flowers" intended for the Grove in 1771.

*Viola tricolor*   "Tricolor"   Johnny-jump-up, Heartsease
When Jefferson sowed "Tricolor" at Shadwell in the spring of 1767 he was referring to this European native, an endearing flower cultivated for centuries and one of the parents of our modern pansies. The Johnny-jump-up will seed itself and appear in such unexpected places as to charm the soberest of gardeners.

*Watsonia meriana*   Bugle lily
This was another greenhouse bulb, native to the "Cape of Good Hope," sent by McMahon in 1812. None of the South African bulbs sent by McMahon enjoy much popularity presently, although the freesia, which is similar in habitat and appearance, is very popular today as a fragrant and colorful florist's flower. It was not introduced until later in the nineteenth century.

*Zephyranthes atamasco*    Atamasco lily
Bulbs of this early-blooming wildflower were forwarded by
McMahon in 1812 to Monticello. The atamasco lily is native
to the woodlands of the southeast and has large lilylike white
flowers, which gradually turn pink. One-quarter of the flowers grown at Monticello were native to North America. This
is a rather high percentage and reflects Jefferson's sensitivity
to the bounties of his own country.

 *Doctor Say will hand your excellency a small packet con-
taining a few seeds of a beautiful flowering tree together
with a Catalogue of our collection. The tree is the Mimosa julibrescens (Silk tree) a native of Persia and Ar-
menia; lately brought to us by the celebrated Michaux the
elder. Its delicate sweet flowers grow in fascicles, composed
of a number of slender silky threads tipped with crimson
antherae.*

WILLIAM BARTRAM TO JEFFERSON (1808)

# COMMON NAMES
## ANNUAL AND PERENNIAL FLOWERS

"American columbo"   *Swertia caroliniensis*

Anemone, "double"   *Anemone coronaria* (poppy-flowered anemone) or *A. hortensis*

Auricula   *Primula auricula*

Bachelor button   *Centaurea cyanus*

Balsam, "double"   *Impatiens balsamina*

Balsam apple   *Momordica balsamina*

"Bellflower"   *Campanula medium*

Blue-eyed grass   *Sisyrinchium angustifolia*

Bounting Bet   *Saponaria officinalis*

Calendula   *Calendula officinalis*

Canterbury bell   *Campanula medium*

Cardinal flower   *Lobelia cardinalis*

Carnation   *Dianthus caryophyllus*

Celosia   *Celosia cristata*

"Chinese ixia"   *Belamcanda chinensis*

Chinese lantern   *Physalis alkekengi*

Cloth of gold crocus   *Crocus angustifolia*

Cockscomb   *Celosia cristata*

Columbine, European   *Aquilegia vulgaris*
   wild   *Aquilegia canadensis*

Cornflower   *Centaurea cyanus*

Crocus, cloth of gold   *Crocus angustifolia*
   Dutch   *C. vernus*
   saffron   *C. sativus*
   spring   *C. vernus*

Cypress vine   *Ipomoea quamoclit*

Daffodil   *Narcissus sp.*

"Daisy"   *Bellis perennis*

"Dragon's tongue"   *Chimaphila maculata*

English daisy   *Bellis perennis*

"European winter cherry"   *Physalis alkekengi*

"Flag"   *Iris germanica*

Fleur-de-lis   *Iris pseudoacorus*

"Flower-de-luces"   *Iris pseudoacorus*

Four-o'clock   *Mirabilis jalapa*

"Fraxinella"   *Dictamnus albus*

French marigold   *Tagetes patula*

"French pink bleuette"   *Centaurea cyanus*

Fritillaria   *Fritillaria imperialis*

Gas plant   *Dictamnus albus*

Geranium   *Pelargonium inquinans* or *P. zonale*

"Gilliflower"   *Dianthus caryophyllus* or *Matthiola incana*

Gladiolus   *Gladiolus communis*

Globe amaranth   *Gomphrena globosa*

Globeflower   *Trollius europaeus*

Golden crownbeard   *Verbesina encelioides*

Heartsease   *Viola tricolor*

Heliotrope   *Heliotropium arborescens*

Hollyhock   *Alcea rosea*

Honesty   *Lunaria annua*

Hyacinth   *Hyacinthus orientalis*
  feathered   *Muscari comosum* var.
    *monstrosum*

Ice plant   *Mesembryanthemum crystallinum*
Iris, Bearded   *Iris germanica*
  "dwarf Persian"   *I. persica*
  German   *I. germanica*
  Spanish   *I. xiphium*
  yellow   *I. pseudoacorus*

Jeffersonia   *Jeffersonia diphylla*
Jerusalem cherry   *Solanum pseudocapsicum*
Johnny-jump-up   *Viola tricolor*
Jonquil   *Narcissus* sp. or *N. jonquilla*
Joseph's coat   *Amaranthus tricolor*

Larkspur   *Consolida orientalis*
  American   *Delphinium exaltatum*
Lady slipper orchid, pink   *Cypripedium acaule*
  yellow   *C. calceolus* var. *pubescens*
Lily, "atamasco"   *Zephyranthes atamasco*
  belladonna   *Amaryllis belladonna*
  blackberry   *Belamcanda chinensis*
  bugle   *Watsonia meriana*
  Canadian   *Lilium canadense*
  "Columbian"   *Fritillaria pudica*
  crown imperial   *Fritillaria imperialis*
  "fiery"   *Lilium chalcedonicum*
  Jacobean   *Sprekelia formosissima*
  Madonna   *Lilium candidum*
  scarlet turk's cap   *Lilium chalcedonicum*
  "Turk's cap"   *Lilium superbum*

  "white"   *Lilium candidum*
Lily of the valley   *Convallaria majalis*
Love-lies-bleeding   *Amaranthus caudatus*
"Lunaria"   *Lunaria annua*
"Lychnis"   *Lychnis chalcedonica* or *L. coronaria*
  "scarlet"   *L. chalcedonica*

Mallow, "eastern"   unidentified
  "French"   *Malva sylvestris*
  "the shrub marshmallow"   *Lavatera olbia*
  "scarlet"   *Pentapetes phoenicia*
Maltese cross   *Lychnis chalcedonica*
Marigold, African   *Tagetes erecta*
  French   *T. patula*
Marshmallow   *Althaea officinalis*
  "shrub"   *Lavatera olbia*
Martagon, "Alleghany"   *Lilium superbum*
  "Canada"   *Lilium canadense*
"Marygold"   *Calendula officinalis*
Mayapple   *Podyphyllum peltatum*
Mignonette   *Reseda odorata*
"Mockaseen"   *Cypripedium acaule*
Money plant   *Lunaria annua*
"Mountain cowslip"   *Mertensia virginica*
"Mourning bride"   unidentified

Narcissus   *Narcissus* sp.
Nasturtium   *Tropaeolum majus*
Native columbine   *Aquilegia canadensis*
Nigella   *Nigella sativa*
"Nutmeg plant"   *Nigella sativa*

"Pasque flower"   *Anemone pulsatilla*

Pea, "Arkansas"   *Lupinus subcarnosus*
  "everlasting"   *Lathyrus latifolius*
  "Lewis'"   *Lupinus subcarnosus*
  sweet   *Lathyrus odoratus*
Peony   *Paeonia officinalis*
Persian buttercup   *Ranunculus asiaticus*
Pink, "China"   *Dianthus chinensis*
  cottage   *D. plumarius*
  "Indian"   *D. chinensis* or *D. plumarius*
Pipsissewa   *Chimaphila maculata*
Polyanthus   *Primula* × *polyantha*
Poppy, corn   *Papaver rhoeas*
  "double"   *P. rhoeas*
  "dwarf"   *P. rhoeas*
  "larger"   *P. somniferum*
  "lesser"   *P. rhoeas*
  opium   *P. somniferum*
  prickly   *Argemone mexicana*
  "white"   *Papaver somniferum*
  yellow-horned   *Glaucium flavum*
Primrose   *Primula vulgaris*
Prince's-feather   *Amaranthus hybridus* var. *erythrostachys*

Ranunculus, "double"   *Ranunculus asiaticus*

Sensitive plant   *Mimosa pudica*
Snapdragon   *Antirrhinum majus*

Snowdrop   *Galanthus nivalis*
Snowflake   *Leucojum* sp.
Soapwort   *Saponaria officinalis*
Spotted wintergreen   *Chimaphila maculata*
"Star of Bethlehem"   *Hypoxis hirsuta*
Stock   *Matthiola incana*
Sunflower   *Helianthus annuus* or *H. divaricatus*
Sweet William   *Dianthus barbatus*

Texas bluebonnet   *Lupinus subcarnosus*
Tree lavatera   *Lavatera olbia*
"Tricolor"   *Viola tricolor*
Tuberose, "double"   *Polianthes tuberosa*
Tulip   *Tulipa* sp.
Twinleaf   *Jeffersonia diphylla*

Venus flytrap   *Dionaea muscipula*
Violet   *Viola* sp.
  "Dutch"   *Viola* sp.
Virginia bluebell   *Mertensia virginica*

Wallflower   *Cheiranthus cheiri*

Yellow stargrass   *Hypoxis hirsuta*
Yellow fritillary   *Fritillaria pudica*

# A List of Woody Ornamentals
# Grown by Jefferson

The following list of ornamental plants grown by Thomas Jefferson is arranged alphabetically and is divided into two sections; the first is a list of trees, shrubs, vines, and roses arranged according to their botanical names, and the second is a compilation of all the woody ornamentals alphabetized by their common names. Quotation marks surround names used by Jefferson.

## TREES

*Abies alba*   Silver fir
*Abies balsamea*   "Balm of Gilead fir"   Balsam fir
*Acer pseudoplatanus*   Sycamore maple
*Acer rubrum*   "Scarlet flowering maple"   Red maple
*Acer saccharum*   Sugar maple
*Acer tataricum*   Tatarian maple
*Aesculus hippocastanum*   European horse chestnut
*Aesculus octandra*   "Yellow horse chestnut," "Aesculus virginica"   Yellow buckeye
*Aesculus pavia*   "Scarlet horse chestnut"   Red buckeye
*Albizia julibrissin*   "Chinese silk tree"   Mimosa

*Amelanchier canadensis*   "Service tree"   Shadblow
*Arbutus unedo*   Strawberry tree
*Artocarpus altilis*   Breadfruit tree
*Asimina triloba*   Pawpaw

*Broussonetia papyrifera*   "Otaheite," "Paper tree"   Paper mulberry

*Carpinus caroliniana*   "Hornbeam"   Ironwood
*Carya illinoinensis*   "Paccan"   Pecan
*Carya laciniosa*   Shellbark hickory
*Carya ovata*   Shagbark hickory
*Carya* sp.   Gloucester hickory
*Carya* sp.
*Castanea dentata*   American chestnut

*Castanea sativa* "French chestnut," "Marronier" European chestnut

*Catalpa bignonioides* Catalpa

*Cedrus libani* Cedar of Lebanon

*Ceratonia siliqua* Carob tree

*Cercis canadensis* Redbud

*Chamaecyparis thyoides* White cedar

*Chionanthus virginica* "Snowdrop tree" Fringe tree

*Citrus aurantifolia* Lime

*Citrus aurantium* Sour orange

*Cornus florida* Dogwood

*Cornus mas* "Ciriege corniole" Cornelian cherry

*Corylus americana* "Hazel" Hazelnut

*Crataegus crus-galli* Cockspur hawthorn

*Crataegus laevigata* "Thorn haws from Algiers" English hawthorn

*Crataegus phaenopyrum* "Thorn haws" Washington hawthorn

*Diospyros virginiana* Persimmon

*Euonymus europaea* European spindle tree

*Fagus grandifolia* "Beach" American beech

*Fagus sylvatica* var. *atropunicea* "Purple beech" Copper beech

*Firmiana simplex* Chinese parasol tree

*Fraxinus americana* White ash

*Fraxinus excelsior* European ash

*Ginkgo biloba* Ginkgo

*Gleditsia triacanthos* "Kentucky locust" Honey locust

*Gymnocladus dioica* Kentucky coffee tree

*Halesia carolina* Silver bell

*Ilex aquifolium* English holly

*Ilex opaca* American holly

*Ilex vomitoria* "Cassioberry," "Cassine" Yaupon holly

*Juglans nigra* Black walnut

*Juglans regia* "French walnut," "Madeira walnut" English walnut

*Juniperus virginiana* Red cedar

*Koelreuteria paniculata* Goldenrain tree

*Laburnum anagyroides* Goldenchain tree

*Larix decidua* "Italian larch" European larch

*Liriodendron tulipifera* Tulip poplar

*Maclura pomifera* "Bow wood," "Osage apple" Osage orange

*Magnolia acuminata* "Cucumber tree" Cucumber magnolia

*Magnolia grandiflora* Southern magnolia

*Magnolia tripetala* "Umbrella" Umbrella magnolia

*Magnolia virginiana* "Swamp laurel," "Magnolia glauca" Sweet bay

*Malus coronaria* "Wild crab" Wild sweet crab

*Malus sylvestris* European crab-apple

*Melia azedarach* "Pride of China," "Beadtree" Chinaberry

*Morus alba* White mulberry

*Morus nigra* "English mulberry" Black mulberry

*Morus rubra* Red mulberry

*Myroxylon balsamum* var. *pereirae* Balsam of Peru


*Olea europaea* Olive


*Picea abies* "Norway fir" Norway spruce

*Picea glauca* "Large silver fir" White spruce

*Picea mariana* "Newfoundland fir" Black spruce

*Pinus rigida* Pitch pine

*Pinus strobus* "Weymouth pine" White pine

*Pinus sylvestris* Scotch pine

*Platanus* × *acerifolia* London plane tree

*Platanus occidentalis* "Plane-tree" Sycamore

*Populus balsamifera* "Tacamahac" Balsam poplar

*Populus deltoides* "Cotton tree" Cottonwood

*Populus* × *gileadensis* Balm of Gilead

*Populus nigra* var. *italica* Lombardy poplar

*Populus tremula* "Monticello aspen" European aspen

*Populus tremuloides* Aspen

*Prunus avium* Sweet cherry

*Prunus cerasus* "Dwarf cherry" Sour cherry

*Prunus persica* "Double flowered peach"

*Prunus serotina* Black cherry

*Prunus virginiana* "Choak cherry" Wild cherry


*Quercus coccifera* "Prickly Kermes" Kermes oak

*Quercus ilicifolia* "Ground oak," "Dwarf oak" Bear oak

*Quercus phellos* Willow oak

*Quercus robur* English oak

*Quercus suber* "Cork tree" Cork oak


*Robinia pseudoacacia* "Common locust," "Locust" Black locust

*Robinia viscosa* "Red locust" Clammy locust


*Salix alba* var. *vitellina* "Golden willow" Yellow weeping willow

*Salix babylonica* Weeping willow

*Sassafras albidum* Sassafras

*Sorbus aucuparia* "Mountain ash" European mountain ash


*Taxus baccata* English yew

*Taxus canadensis* "Dwarf yew" American yew

*Thuja occidentalis* Arborvitae

*Thuja orientalis* Chinese arborvitae

*Tilia americana* American linden or Basswood

*Tilia* sp. "Linden"

*Tsuga canadensis* "Hemlock spruce" Canadian hemlock

*Ulmus americana*    "Elm"    American elm
*Ulmus procera*    English elm

*Viburnum prunifolium*    "Haw"    Black haw

*Virgilia capensis*

*Zanthoxylum americanum*    Prickly ash
*Zizyphus jujuba*    Common jujube

## SHRUBS

*Acacia farnesiana*    "*Acacia nilotica*"    Sweet acacia
*Alnus rugosa*    Alder
*Amorpha fruticosa*    Bastard indigo

*Berberis vulgaris*    European barberry

*Callicarpa americana*    "Callicarpa"    Beauty-berry
*Calycanthus floridus*    "Bubby flower shrub"    Sweet shrub
*Castanea pumila*    Chinquapin
*Ceanothus americanus*    New Jersey tea
*Clethra alnifolia*    Sweet pepper bush
*Colutea arborescens*    Bladder senna
*Cornus sanguinea*    "Dogberry"    Swamp dogwood
*Coronilla emerus*    Scorpion senna
*Cotinus coggygria*    "Venetian sumach"    Smoke tree
*Cytisus scoparius*    Scotch broom

*Daphne cneorum*    Rose daphne
*Daphne mezereum*    "Mezereon"

*Euonymus americanus*    "Euonymus sempervirens," "Evergreen spindle tree"    Strawberry bush

*Gardenia jasminoides*    "Cape jasmine"    Gardenia

*Hibiscus syriacus*    "Althaea"    Rose of Sharon

*Ilex verticillata*    Winterberry

*Jasminum officinale*    "Jasmine," "White jasmine," "Star jasmine"

*Kalmia latifolia*    "Ivy," "Dwarf laurel"    Mountain laurel

*Ligustrum vulgare*    Common privet

*Nerium oleander*   Oleander

*Philadelphus coronarius*   Mock orange
*Prunus triloba*   "Amygdalus flore pleno," "Double blossomed almond"   Flowering almond
*Pyracantha coccinea*   "Mespilus," "Prickly medlar"   Pyracantha
*Pyrularia pubera*   "Oil shrub" Buffalo nut

*Rhododendron maximum*   "Rosebay"   Rosebay rhododendron
*Rhododendron periclymenoides* "Wild honeysuckle"   Pinxter azalea
*Ribes aureum*   "Lewis' yellow currant"   Golden currant
*Ribes odoratum*   "Lewis' sweet-scented currant"   Buffalo currant

*Robinia hispida*   "Prickly locust" Moss locust

*Sambucus canadensis*   "Elder" Elderberry
*Spartium junceum*   Spanish broom
*Symphoricarpos albus*   Snowberry
*Syringa persica*   "Persian jasmine" Persian lilac
*Syringa vulgaris*   Common lilac

*Taxus canadensis*   "Dwarf yew" American yew

*Ulex europaeus*   "Furze"   Gorse

*Viburnum opulus* var. *sterile* "Snowball," "Guelder rose" Snowball bush
*Viburnum trilobum*   "Bush cranberry"
*Vitex agnus-castus*   Chaste tree

## VINES

*Campsis radicans*   "Trumpet flower"   Trumpet vine
*Clematis virginiana*   Virgin's bower

*Gelsemium sempervirens*   "Yellow jasmine"

*Hedysarum coronarium*   "Scarlet monthly honeysuckle" French honeysuckle

*Lonicera alpigena*   "Red berried honeysuckle"

*Lonicera sempervirens*   "Trumpet honeysuckle"   Coral honeysuckle

*Rhus toxicodendron*   "Poison oak" Poison ivy

*Vinca minor*   Periwinkle

*Wisteria frutescens*   "Carolina kidney bean tree with purple flowers"   Wisteria

## ROSES

*Rosa* × *alba*  "White damask," "White rose"

*Rosa centifolia* 'Major'  "Large Provence rose"  Great double Holland rose

*Rosa centifolia* var. *muscosa* 'Communis'  "Moss Provence rose"  Common moss

*Rosa cinnamomea*  Cinnamon rose

*Rosa damascena* 'Bifera' "Monthly"  Autumn damask

*Rosa eglanteria*  Sweetbriar rose

*Rosa foetida* 'Lutea'  "Yellow rose"  Austrian yellow rose

*Rosa gallica* 'Versicolor'  "Rosa mundi"

*Rosa laevigata*  Cherokee rose

*Rosa moschata*  Musk rose

*Rosa officinalis*  "Crimson dwarf rose"

*Rosa pendulina*  "Thornless rose"

*Rosa spinosissima*  "Primrose"  Burnet or Scotch hedge rose

## COMMON NAMES
### TREES, SHRUBS, VINES, AND ROSES

"*Acacia nilotica*"  *Acacia farnesiana*

Alder  *Alnus rugosa*

Almond, "double blossomed"  *Prunus triloba*

flowering  *P. trilboa*

"Althaea"  *Hibiscus syriacus*

Arborvitae, American  *Thuja occidentalis*

Chinese  *T. orientalis*

Ash, European  *Fraxinus excelsior*

European mountain  *Sorbus aucuparia*

"mountain"  *S. aucuparia*

prickly  *Zanthoxylum americanum*

white  *Fraxinus americana*

Aspen *Populus tremuloides*

European  *P. tremula*

"Monticello"  *P. tremula*

Balm of Gilead  *Populus* × *gileadensis*

Balsam of Peru  *Myroxylon balsamum* var. *pereirae*

Barberry, European  *Berberis vulgaris*

Basswood  *Tilia americana*

Bastard indigo  *Amorpha fruticosa*

"Beach"  *Fagus grandifolia*

"Beadtree"  *Melia azedarach*

Beauty-berry  *Callicarpa americana*

Beech, American  *Fagus grandifolia*

copper  *F. sylvatica* var. *atropunicea*

"purple"  *F. sylvatica* var. *atropunicea*

Bladder senna  *Colutea arborescens*

"Bow wood"  *Maclura pomifera*

Breadfruit tree  *Artocarpus altilis*

"Bubby flower shrub"  *Calycanthus floridus*

Buckeye, red  *Aesculus pavia*

yellow  *A. octandra*

Buffalo nut  *Pyrularia pubera*

"Bush cranberry"    *Viburnum trilobum*

"Callicarpa"    *Callicarpa americana*
Carob tree    *Ceratonia siliqua*
"Carolina kidney bean tree with purple flowers"    *Wisteria frutescens*
"Cassine"    *Ilex vomitoria*
"Cassioberry"    *Ilex vomitoria*
Catalpa    *Catalpa bignonioides*
Cedar, of Lebanon    *Cedrus libani*
    red    *Juniperus virginiana*
    white    *Chamaecyparis thyoides*
Chaste tree    *Vitex agnus-castus*
Cherry, black    *Prunus serotina*
    "choak"    *P. virginiana*
    cornelian    *Cornus mas*
    "dwarf"    *Prunus cerasus*
    sour    *P. cerasus*
    sweet    *P. avium*
    wild    *P. virginiana*
Chestnut, American    *Castanea dentata*
    European    *C. sativa*
    "French"    *C. sativa*
Chinaberry    *Melia azedarach*
Chinese parasol tree    *Firmiana simplex*
"Chinese silk tree"    "Albizia julibrissin"
Chinquapin    *Castanea pumila*
"Ciriege corniole"    *Cornus mas*
"Cork tree"    *Quercus suber*
"Cotton tree"    *Populus deltoides*
Cottonwood    *Populus deltoides*
Crabapple, European    *Malus sylvestris*
    wild sweet    *M. coronaria*
"Cucumber tree"    *Magnolia acuminata*
Currant, buffalo    *Ribes odoratum*

golden    *R. aureum*
"Lewis' sweetscented"    *R. odoratum*
"Lewis' yellow"    *R. aureum*

"Dogberry"    *Cornus sanguinea*
Dogwood    *Cornus florida*
    swamp    *C. sanguinea*

Elm, American    *Ulmus americana*
    English    *U. procera*
"Elder"    *Sambucus canadensis*
Elderberry    *Sambucus canadensis*

Fir, "balm of Gilead"    *Abies balsamea*
    balsam    *A. balsamea*
    "large silver"    *Picea glauca*
    "Newfoundland"    *P. mariana*
    "Norway"    *P. abies*
    silver    *Abies alba*
Fringe tree    *Chionanthus virginica*
"Furze"    *Ulex europaeus*

Gardenia    *Gardenia jasminoides*
Ginkgo    *Ginkgo biloba*
Golden chain tree    *Laburnum anagyroides*
Goldenrain tree    *Koelreuteria paniculata*
Gorse    *Ulex europaeus*
"Guelder rose"    *Viburnum opulus* var. *sterile*

"Haw"    *Viburnum prunifolium*
    black    *V. prunifolium*
Hawthorn, cockspur    *Crataegus crus-galli*
    English    *C. laevigata*
    Washington    *C. phaenopyrum*
"Hazel"    *Corylus americana*
Hazelnut    *Corylus americana*

Hemlock, Canadian *Tsuga canadensis*
"Hemlock spruce" *Tsuga canadensis*
Hickory, Gloucester *Carya* sp.
  shagbark *C. ovata*
  Shellbark *C. laciniosa*
Holly, American *Ilex opaca*
  English *I. aquifolium*
  yaupon *I. vomitoria*
Honeysuckle, coral *Lonicera sempervirens*
  French *Hedysarum coronarium*
  "red-berried" *Lonicera alpigena*
  "scarlet monthly" *Hedysarum coronarium*
  "trumpet" *Lonicera sempervirens*
  "wild" *Rhododendron periclymenoides*
"Hornbeam" *Carpinus caroliniana*
Horse chestnut, European *Aesculus hippocastanum*
  "scarlet" *A. pavia*
  "yellow" *A. octandra*

Ironwood *Carpinus caroliniana*
"Ivy" *Kalmia latifolia*

"Jasmine" *Jasminum officinale*
  "Cape" *Gardenia jasminoides*
  "Persian" *Syringa persica*
  "star" *Jasminum officinale*
  "white" *J. officinale*
  "yellow" *Gelsemium sempervirens*
Jujube *Ziziphus jujuba*

Kentucky coffee tree *Gymnocladus dioica*

Larch, European *Larix decidua*
  "Italian" *L. decidua*

Laurel, "dwarf" *Kalmia latifolia*
  mountain *K. latifolia*
  "swamp" *Magnolia virginiana*
Lilac, common *Syringa vulgaris*
  Persian *S. persica*
Lime *Citrus aurantifolia*
Linden *Tilia* sp.
  American *Tilia americana*
Locust, black *Robinia pseudoacacia*
  clammy *R. viscosa*
  "common" *R. pseudoacacia*
  honey *Gleditsia triacanthos*
  "Kentucky" *G. triacanthos*
  moss *Robinia hispida*
  "prickly" *R. hispida*
  red *R. viscosa*
London plane tree *Platanus* × *acerifolia*

Magnolia, cucumber *Magnolia acuminata*
  "glauca" *M. virginiana*
  southern *M. grandiflora*
  sweet bay *M. virginiana*
  umbrella *M. tripetala*
Maple, red *Acer rubrum*
  "scarlet flowering" *A. rubrum*
  sugar *A. saccharum*
  sycamore *A. pseudoplatanus*
  Tatarian *A. tataricum*
"Marronier" *Castanea sativa*
"Mespilus" *Pyracantha coccinea*
"Mezereon" *Daphne mezereum*
Mimosa *Albizia julibrissin*
Mock orange *Philadelphus coronarius*
Mulberry, black *Morus nigra*
  "English" *M. nigra*
  paper *Broussonetia papyrifera*
  red *Morus rubra*
  white *M. alba*

New Jersey tea    *Ceanothus americanus*

Oak, bear    *Quercus ilicifolia*
  cork    *Q. suber*
  "dwarf"    *Q. ilicifolia*
  English    *Q. robur*
  "ground"    *Q. ilicifolia*
  kermes    *Q. coccifera*
  "poison"    *Rhus toxicodendron*
  willow    *Quercus phellos*
"Oil shrub"    *Pyrularia pubera*
Oleander    *Nerium oleander*
Olive    *Olea europaea*
Orange, mock    *Philadelphus coron-
arius*
  Osage    *Maclura pomifera*
  sour    *Citrus aurantium*
"Osage apple"    *Maclura pomifera*
Osage orange    *Maclura pomifera*
"Otaheite"    *Broussonetia papyrifera*

"Paccan"    *Carya illinoinensis*
"Paper tree"    *Broussonetia papyri-
fera*
Pawpaw    *Asimina triloba*
Peach, "double flowered"    *Prunus
persica*
Pecan    *Carya illinoinensis*
Periwinkle    *Vinca minor*
Persimmon    *Diospyros virginiana*
Pine, pitch    *Pinus rigida*
  Scotch    *P. sylvestris*
  "Weymouth"    *P. strobus*
  white    *P. strobus*
Pinxter azalea    *Rhododendron peri-
clymenoides*
"Plane-tree"    *Platanus occidentalis*
Poison ivy    *Rhus toxicodendron*
"Poison oak"    *Rhus toxicodendron*
Poplar, balsam    *Populus balsamifera*
  Lombardy    *P. nigra* var. *italica*

tulip    *Liriodendron tulipifera*
  yellow    *L. tulipifera*
"Prickly kermes"    *Quercus coccifera*
"Prickly medlar"    *Pyracantha cocci-
nea*
"Pride of China"    *Melia azedarach*
"Primrose"    *Rosa spinosissima*
Privet    *Ligustrum vulgare*
Pyracantha    *Pyracantha coccinea*

Redbud    *Cercis canadensis*
"Rosa mundi"    *Rosa gallica* 'Versicolor'
Rose, Austrian yellow    *Rosa foetida* 'Lutea'
  autumn damask    *R. damascena*
  'Bifera'
  Burnet    *R. spinosissima*
  Cherokee    *R. laevigata*
  Cinnamon    *R. cinnamomea*
  "crimson dwarf"    *R. officinalis*
  great double Holland    *R. centifolia* 'Major'
  "large Provence"    *R. centifolia*
  'Major'
  "monthly"    *R. damascena* 'Bifera'
  moss    *R. centifolia* var. *muscosa*
  'Communis'
  "moss Provence"    *R. centifolia*
  var. *muscosa* 'Communis'
  musk    *R. moschata*
  "Primrose"    *R. spinosissima*
  "rosa mundi"    *R. gallica* 'Versicolor'
  Scotch hedge    *R. spinosissima*
  sweetbriar    *R. eglanteria*
  "thornless"    *R. pendulina*
  "white damask"    *R.* × *alba*
  "yellow"    *R. foetida* 'Lutea'
Rosebay rhododendron    *Rhododendron maximum*

Rose daphne     *Daphne cneorum*
Rose of Sharon     *Hibiscus syriacus*

Sassafras     *Sassafras albidum*
Scorpion senna     *Coronilla emerus*
Scotch broom     *Cytisus scoparius*
"Service tree"     *Amelanchier cana-
    densis*
Shadblow     *Amelanchier canadensis*
Silver bell     *Halesia carolina*
Smoke tree     *Cotinus coggygria*
"Snowball"     *Viburnum opulus* var.
    *sterile*
Snowberry     *Symphoricarpos albus*
Snowdrop tree     *Chionanthus vir-
    ginica*
Spanish broom     *Spartium junceum*
Spindle tree, European     *Euonymus
    europaea*
    "evergreen"     *E. americanus*
Spruce, black     *Picea mariana*
    "hemlock"     *Tsuga canadensis*
    Norway     *Picea abies*
    white     *P. glauca*
Strawberry bush     *Euonymus amer-
    icanus*
Strawberry tree     *Arbutus unedo*
Sweet acacia     *Acacia farnesiana*
Sweet bay     *Magnolia virginiana*
Sweet pepper bush     *Clethra alni-
    folia*
Sweet shrub     *Calycanthus floridus*

Sycamore     *Platanus occidentalis*

"Tacamahac"     *Populus balsamifera*
"Thorn haws"     *Crataegus phaeno-
    pyrum*
"Thorn haws from Algiers"     *Cra-
    taegus laevigata*
"Trumpet flower"     *Campsis radi-
    cans*
Trumpet vine     *Campsis radicans*

"Umbrella"     *Magnolia tripetala*

"Venetian sumach"     *Cotinus cog-
    gygria*
Virgin's bower     *Clematis virginiana*

Walnut, black     *Juglans nigra*
    English     *J. regia*
    "French"     *J. regia*
    "Madeira"     *J. regia*
Weeping willow     *Salix babylonica*
    yellow     *S. alba* var. *vitellina*
Willow, "golden"     *Salix alba* var.
    *vitellina*
Winterberry     *Ilex verticillata*
Wisteria     *Wisteria frutescens*

Yew, American     *Taxus canadensis*
    "dwarf"     *T. canadensis*
    English     *T. baccata*

*A 'propos of plants, make a thousand acknolegements in my name and with my respects to Mrs. Bankhead for the favor proposed of the Cape Jessamine. It will be cherished with all the possible attentions: and in return proffer her Calycanthuses, Paccans, Silk trees, Canada martagons or any thing else we have.*
JEFFERSON TO ANNE CARY RANDOLPH BANKHEAD (1809)

# Bibliography

## BOOKS AND PAMPHLETS

Bear, James A., Jr., ed., *Jefferson at Monticello:* Memoirs of a Monticello Slave *as dictated to Charles Campbell by Isaac, and* Jefferson at Monticello: The Private Life of Thomas Jefferson *by Rev. Hamilton Wilcox Pierson*. Charlottesville, Va., 1967.

Betts, Edwin Morris, ed., *Thomas Jefferson's Farm Book*. 1953; repr. Charlottesville, Va., 1976.

——, *Thomas Jefferson's Garden Book, 1766–1824*. Philadelphia, 1944.

Betts, Edwin Morris, and James Adam Bear, Jr., eds. *The Family Letters of Thomas Jefferson*. Columbia, Mo., 1966.

Bixby, William K., *Thomas Jefferson's Correspondence*. 1916.

Boyd, Julian P., ed., *The Papers of Thomas Jefferson*. Princeton, N.J., 1950–.

Coats, Alice M., *Flowers and Their Histories*. London, 1956.

Foley, John P., *The Jeffersonian Cyclopedia*. 1900; repr. New York, 1967.

*Hortus Third*. Revised and expanded by the staff of the L. H. Bailey Hortorium. New York, 1976.

Jefferson, Thomas, *Notes on the State of Virginia*. 1787; ed. William Peden, Chapel Hill, N.C., 1955.

Kimball, Fiske, *Jefferson's Grounds and Gardens at Monticello*. 1927.

——, *Thomas Jefferson, Architect*. 1916; 2nd ed., New York, 1968.

Leighton, Ann, *American Gardens in the Eighteenth Century*. Boston, 1976.

Lipscomb, A. A., and A. E. Bergh, eds., *The Writings of Thomas Jefferson*. 1903.

McMahon, Bernard, *The American Gardener's Calendar*. 1806.

Malone, Dumas, *Jefferson and His Time*. Boston, 1948–81.

Mayo, Bernard, *Jefferson Himself: The Personal Narrative of a Many-Sided American*. 1942; repr. Charlottesville, Va., 1970.

Miller, Philip, *The Gardener's Dictionary*. 1731; repr. New York, 1968.

Parkinson, John, *Paradisi in Sole: Paradisus terrestris*. London, 1629; repr. New York, 1976.

Peterson, Merrill D., *Thomas Jefferson and the New Nation: A Biography*. New York, 1970.

Randall, Henry S., *Life of Thomas Jefferson*. 1858.

Randolph, Sarah N., *The Domestic Life of Thomas Jefferson*. 1871; repr. New York, 1969.

Sadler, Elizabeth Hatcher, *The Bloom of Monticello*. 1926.
Smith, Margaret Bayard, *The First Forty Years of Washington Society*. 1906;
 repr. New York, 1965.
Sprague, Isaac, and Asa Gray, *The Genera of the Plants of the United States*.
 1848.
*Transactions of the American Philosophical Society*, 3 (1793):342.
Tucker, George, *Life of Thomas Jefferson*. 1837.
Whately, Thomas, *Observations on Modern Gardening*. 1770.
*William and Mary College Quarterly*, 2d ser., 6 (1929):334–35.

## MANUSCRIPTS

Jefferson's Account Books and Memorandum Books: The Library of Congress, Washington, D.C.; The Massachusetts Historical Society, Boston, Massachusetts; The Henry E. Huntington Library, San Marino, California; New York City Public Library; The New-York Historical Society.
Jefferson's Farm Book and Garden Book: The Massachusetts Historical Society.
Jefferson's Scrapbook: Alderman Library, University of Virginia.
Jefferson's Weather Memorandum Book: The Library of Congress.
Letters and Memoranda from and to Jefferson: Alderman Library, University of Virginia; The Henry E. Huntington Library; The Library of Congress; The Massachusetts Historical Society.
Letters of Cornelia Randolph to Ellen Coolidge and Virginia Randolph Trist to Ellen Coolidge: Alderman Library, University of Virginia.
Original Plans of the Garden: The Historical Society of Pennsylvania, Philadelphia; The Massachusetts Historical Society.
Photostatic copies of the above manuscripts are available in the Alderman Library, University of Virginia.